Building America's Hangar

The Design and Construction of
the Steven F. Udvar-Hazy Center

This book is dedicated to members of the core team
who did not live to see our dreams realized at Dulles:

Derwin Abston
Donald D. Engen
Charles Howard
Francis P. Tunstall

First published in 2004 by GILES
an imprint of D Giles Limited
57 Abingdon Road, London, W8 6AN, UK
www.gilesltd.com

ISBN: 1 904832 07 5

All measurements are in metric and English;
height precedes width precedes depth.

For The Smithsonian Institution, National Air and Space Museum:

Lin Ezell, Project Coordinator, National Air and Space Museum,
Steven F. Udvar-Hazy Center

Patricia J. Graboske, Publications Officer,
Smithsonian Institution, National Air and Space Museum

For GILES:
Copy Editor: David Rose
Designed by Mercer Design, London
Produced by GILES, an imprint of D Giles Limited
Printed and bound in China

Photographs are by staff photographers,
contractors, and others as noted.

Front cover: Aviation hangar at sunrise
Back cover: View of *Enola Gay* during installation
of aircraft in aviation hangar
Page 9: June 04 aerial

Building America's Hangar

The Design and Construction of the Steven F. Udvar-Hazy Center

Lin Ezell

Smithsonian Institution, National Air and Space Museum, Washington, D.C. in association with D Giles Limited, London

Made possible through a generous donation by Hensel Phelps Construction Company

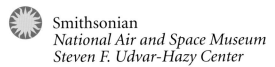
Smithsonian
National Air and Space Museum
Steven F. Udvar-Hazy Center

GILES

Contents

Foreword

Donald S. Lopez is a World War II veteran aviator and ace. He flew P-40s in the China-Burma-India theater. *Lope's Hope* is on display at the Udvar-Hazy Center.

THERE IS NO ONE better qualified to record the history of the construction of the Steven F. Udvar-Hazy Center of the National Air and Space Museum than Lin Ezell. She is not only a gifted writer, but she was with the project from before the get-go, this being when President Clinton signed the bill authorizing construction of the new Museum annex in 1993.

Lin was uniquely prepared for her role as coordinator of the project. She had served NASM as a curator and, more importantly, spent 10 years as head of the restoration department, little knowing at the time that she would play such a key role in the creation of the facility to house the very artifacts they were restoring. She took on the daunting task of coordinating the major architectural and construction project in 1996. She spent many months in almost daily meetings with the architects, Hellmuth, Obata + Kassabaum, helping to ensure that the Museum's requirements took precedence over the architect's natural concern over the building's aesthetics. Fortunately, the architects were able to do both, creating a handsome and very functional facility. She worked with the architects to shepherd the design through the National Capital Planning Commission and the Commission of Fine Arts.

Lin was a member of the committee that evaluated the proposals of the companies that were bidding for the construction contract. The selection of Hensel Phelps Construction Company as the prime contractor was one of the major reasons that the project ran so smoothly and was completed on time and under budget. They were more like partners than contractors. Once construction began, Lin spent the next few years working out of the construction trailers as NASM's representative on the project, driving every day from southern Maryland to the Dulles site.

It was a great personal satisfaction to me to see the Hazy Center Project come to fruition. I had long been working toward getting a building to house the many artifacts that would not fit into the Mall Museum. I have been at NASM since 1972 and was deeply involved in opening the Mall Museum. It was apparent from that time that a much larger museum on an active airport would be required for our collection. I am especially glad to see a P-40 in my 75th Fighter Squadron markings hanging proudly in the entrance overlook.

Lin's book, *Building America's Hangar*, covers succinctly, but clearly, the many twists and turns of this project as the museum struggled to obtain its approval, the many details involved in completing the design, and the challenges of the construction. In addition to the good writing, the many well-captioned photographs not only illustrate the story but are a tribute to the many fine photographers on the NASM staff. I recommend this book highly, not only for the Museum's story but as a great example of how a large-scale project is carried out. We almost had to carry Lin out when it was finished.

Donald S. Lopez
Deputy Director, NASM

Introduction

FOR MORE THAN 150 YEARS, the Smithsonian Institution has been sharing the wealth of its collections and the depth of its research with millions of visitors, either firsthand at one of its 26 museums and research facilities or through its outreach programs. At museums, we come face to face with real examples of what we heard about as children—dinosaurs or steam locomotives—or what we actually used in our everyday life—Flash Gordon lunchboxes or kitchen gadgets. Or we finally see for ourselves objects made familiar only through books and television—the spacecraft that brought home the first men from their voyage to the Moon. Or we behold a symbol long held sacred by a free people—the Star Spangled Banner. We have a basic need to see for ourselves these special icons of history, these common reminders of our personal history. Museums help make this happen.

First established as the National Air Museum in 1946, the Smithsonian's National Air and Space Museum did not open until 1976. With its first-year attendance, it became the world's most visited museum—a record it continues to maintain most years. But as grand as this Washington, D.C.-based home of

aviation and spaceflight history is, less than 10 percent of the Museum's artifacts have ever been displayed there at any one time. And the largest aircraft on exhibit—the DC-3—represents technology of the 1930s. And even if we could have built a second Air and Space Museum next to the first, it would have been impossible to bring space shuttles and large airliners through downtown city streets. Even as the Museum opened, its staff was casting an eye in the direction of Washington Dulles Airport in northern Virginia. Wouldn't it be ideal to have a second facility right at an airport with runways on which to bring aircraft in directly and with room enough to protect the collection and let it grow?

This book charts the Museum's journey as it answered that question in the affirmative. Like the first Air and Space Museum, it took several decades to cultivate support and obtain approvals for the Dulles facility. Chapter 1 reviews the mission of the Museum and recounts the challenges of finding the very first home for the National Collection of air and space artifacts. Planning and designing the "Dulles Extension" is the subject of the second chapter, a story of resolve and patience. With Congressional approval and support

from the Commonwealth of Virginia, Chapter 3 prepares the airport site for the "Dulles Center." After so much time spent deliberating and planning, the Smithsonian executed the actual construction of the Steven F. Udvar-Hazy Center at a fast pace indeed, and that story is related in Chapter 4. And finally, the last chapter presents a scrapbook of images that remind us why this project is so very important—the artifacts that represent a century of powered flight and the people who made it possible.

We opened the new museum at Dulles on December 15, 2003. During the first six months, over 1,000,000 visitors found their way to our door. They came to stand next to wood and fabric aircraft that had flown when the age of powered flight was new, when aircraft flew over European skies angry with war. Icons of World War II, from all theaters and most of the combatant nations, were a draw. The Museum finally had enough room at the Udvar-Hazy Center to assemble and exhibit *Enola Gay*, the B-29 bomber that dropped the first atomic weapon, which led to the final surrender of that global war. Large aircraft, like the Concorde and the first Boeing 707, graced the hangar floor, while a legion of planes seemingly flew overhead in the

mammoth space. And would-be astronauts came face to face with a space shuttle. The Smithsonian fully expects the adventure and our popularity to continue. The Center was designed with the expectation that 3 to 4 million visitors would frequent the facility annually, and we are on our way.

The project is not complete. Total build-out calls for 68,400 square meters (760,000 sq ft); we had about two-thirds of that in place for opening day. As you will learn in the chapters that follow, the Museum had to phase the project to keep in sync with the funding stream. As I write, the National Air and Space Museum is actively pursuing the additional monies needed to construct the remaining building blocks of the Center, including the restoration hangar, which will almost put you right at the work benches alongside our restorers. And we are not done moving in! When we opened the doors in December, we had 82 aircraft and over 30 spacecraft in place. We intend to display more than 200 aircraft and more than 100 spacecraft. Thousands of smaller artifacts will also be given a new home at Dulles. This book records the first major step of a work in progress.

Building America's Hangar is not exhaustive. It is not a step-by-step guide to building a museum, although Appendix 5 does share some of my lessons learned. Not every design step or construction process is told with equal weight. There will be many parts of the project that go untold, many important people whose stories and faces will not be found among these pages. It was a huge, complex undertaking, too much for one volume and one author. I told the story as I lived

it, and while my head is still swimming with the details, one person could not absorb it all. Every process was important, every person left their mark. I wish I could have told every story.

The Udvar-Hazy Center may be the most photographed construction site on record, or at least it seemed that way to me as I paged through volumes of slides and clicked my way through scores of compact discs. It is a photogenic building! We were blessed with several talented photographers who regularly recorded our progress, from the last old farm fence post coming down to the crowds arriving on opening day. They shot bare steel going up during blustery winter days, and they slogged through red mud when I asked them to record yet another construction milestone. They were up on lifts, rooftops, and ladders. They captured the morning sun's reflection on glass and metal skin and the moon's grace against stainless-steel sculpture. And they didn't forget the people who made it all happen. This is a story that can be told in pictures or words; I hope you will enjoy both.

In preparing this book, I have tapped many resources. Al Bachmeier and William "Jake" Jacobs were my closest Museum colleagues over the long haul. Their dedication to the Center was unsurpassed. From the Office of Facilities Engineering and Operations, the project was staffed—and I was assisted by—Sheryl Kolasinski, Melinda Humphry Becker, Vince Cogliano, George Golden, David Hay, Don Dormstetter, Derek Ross, and Justin Estoque. From Parsons Brinckerhoff, Paul Dickens was always ready with answers and advice. Manuscript readers kept me on target,

and I thank Don Lopez, Al Bachmeier, and Valerie Neal. Volunteer Bill Doole not only commented on the manuscript but also helped with the monumental task of image management and pulled together appendix material for the book. At Hellmuth, Obata + Kassabaum, Walt Urbanek chased down facts and figures for me. And I thank Hensel Phelps Construction Company for their support of this book. Lastly, if it were not for the great photography produced by Carolyn Russo, Mark Avino, Eric Long, Craig Parham, Duane Lempke, and Dane Penland, there would be no book!

I have told this story from my own perspective as program manager and project coordinator; my views and recollections are my own. But to jog my memory, I relied on official records and documents and have made every attempt to document the project accurately. I represented the Museum in the field during the planning, design, and construction phases. While reviewing materials for the early chapters, I found my name on attendee lists for meetings related to Dulles feasibility studies as early as 1985. In fact, when I joined the National Air and Space Museum in 1984 as an historian, one of my assigned duties was to represent my department in any discussions related to this distant dream of a second public facility. It has been an honor to be part of the team that opened the doors of a truly magnificent facility. I think we've made a difference.

Lin Ezell
Project Coordinator
Steven F. Udvar-Hazy Center
June 2004

CHAPTER 1

Finding a Home for the National Collection

THERE IS SOMETHING UNDENIABLY MAGICAL ABOUT MACHINES THAT FLY. WHILE SCHOLARS FILL TEXTBOOKS WITH ESSENTIAL ENGINEERING AND SCIENTIFIC DATA THAT EXPLAIN THE MECHANICS OF POWERED FLIGHT AND SPACE EXPLORATION, CHILDREN MARVEL AT THE SIMPLE ENORMITY OF A LOW-FLYING AIRLINER AS IT LUMBERS IN FOR A LANDING, POETS ARE INSPIRED BY BOUNDARIES BROKEN BY FLIGHT, AND THOSE OF US WITH OUR FEET FIRMLY ON THE GROUND ENVY THE ASSUMED FREEDOM OF PILOTS, WHO HAVE BEEN ZOOMING OUT OF SIGHT FOR OVER 100 YEARS. THE SMITHSONIAN INSTITUTION BEGAN COLLECTING RELICS RELATED TO FLIGHT EVEN BEFORE THE WRIGHT BROTHERS TOOK OFF UNDER POWER AT KITTY HAWK IN 1903.

Charles A. Lindbergh flew solo non-stop across the Atlantic in 1927, the first person to do so.
He delivered the *Spirit of St. Louis* to the Smithsonian in 1928, where it was exhibited in the National Museum.

Launching the National Air Museum

ESTABLISHED BY CONGRESS in 1846 and initially funded by a $500,000 bequest from British scientist James Smithson, the Smithsonian has consistently sought to broaden our understanding of the world around us. Through basic research in many disciplines and with its vast collections of diverse objects, the Institution reaches broad audiences. In 1882, the Department of Anthropology collected the Smithsonian's first objects related to flight when it acquired 20 Chinese kites that had been part of the 1876 American Centennial Exposition in Philadelphia. With more than a century of flight history to document, by 2004 the Smithsonian's National Air and Space Museum owned more than 51,000 objects, including that collection of exotic 19th century kites. Flying paper dragons were joined by barnstorming aircraft, fighters that waged wars in distant lands, and spacecraft that took men to the Moon.

In 1918, Smithsonian Secretary Charles D. Walcott directed the National Museum to begin collecting aircraft for public display. A metal building near the Smithsonian's Arts and Industries Building, inherited from the War Department, was made available for the aircraft collection and opened to the public two years later. By the time the Institution established the Section of Aeronautics in the Division of Engineering within the Department of Arts and Industries in 1932, the Museum had acquired a significant collection of aircraft, including the *Spirit of St. Louis,*

The War Department transferred a temporary "tin shed," which had been used for testing World War I Liberty engines, to the Smithsonian, where the aviation collection was displayed. It opened to the public in 1920.

the first aircraft to be flown solo non-stop across the Atlantic. At the conclusion of World War II, that collection grew again when examples of Allied and captured enemy aircraft were transferred to the Smithsonian by General of the Army H. H. "Hap" Arnold. General Arnold went on to lobby for the establishment of a National Air Museum where the history of aviation could be preserved at one location. In a letter to the Institute of the Aeronautical Sciences in late 1945, he wrote, "Such a permanent shrine devoted to unparalleled achievements would indeed be a fitting tribute to American aviation and its members who fought so valiantly and successfully in war and in peace to give America preeminence in the air in order that our nation might have peace and security."[1]

Building an Aviation Museum

In 1946, as Smithsonian staff contemplated where to house their new military acquisitions, Congress directed the Institution to establish a new branch, the National Air Museum. The new title did not immediately bring with it new exhibit buildings, but the lawmakers did authorize $50,000 for the new organization. In one of its first acts, the Museum's Advisory Board voted to keep the facility in Washington and started examining some 33 building sites. The Board was looking for 30 to 40 hectares (75–100 acres), accessible and reasonably priced, for a 45,000-square-meter (500,000-sq-ft) building that could house 200 aircraft. In its annual report for 1949, the Museum reported that "Planning and designing a museum building for aircraft and aviation

The Federal Works Agency assisted the Air Museum with its first design studies for a new building in 1949. Project 49.128 detailed a 97,853-square-meter (1,087,260-sq-ft) building with elaborate grounds on 47 hectares (115 acres), complete with an auditorium, cafeteria, a special exhibit area dedicated to the Wright brothers, a large multi-level display hall that measured 238 by 124 meters (780 by 408 ft), and outdoor aircraft storage areas on a nearby concrete apron.

Large aircraft, like the B-29, would be supported on pylons, while smaller aircraft would be perched on two balcony levels, in the 1949 design study.

collections involves factors not usually encountered in museum structures." The designers at the Federal Works Agency, Public Buildings Administration, Office of Design and Construction, were advised that the collections would "include material both of small and uncommonly great dimensions and weight."[2] The Museum was still looking for a suitable site when, in the early 1950s, the Smithsonian was told that the temporary storage haven for its World War II collection near Chicago might soon be taken away, since that Douglas Aircraft factory building might come to life again to manufacture aircraft bound for the Korean War.

Paul Garber, who was the force responsible for building and caring for the Air Museum's collections, found a 8.5-hectare (21-acre) parcel of land in Suitland, Maryland, convenient to Washington but in need of clearing and development so that it could receive the 1,366 "aeronautical objects" coming by train from Illinois, including 97 aircraft. Metal buildings were erected at the "Silver Hill Facility" during the 1950s, but the best efforts by Garber and his team were not sufficient to protect all the objects, some of which would remain outdoors at the site for many years. As the crew labored to store aircraft in Maryland, the Museum acquired and lost a downtown Washington site for the new building but still commissioned an architectural study. Finally, in 1958, three city blocks on the National Mall were set aside for the Air Museum. Five years later, Congress provided funding for the design, and architects at Hellmuth, Obata + Kassabaum set to work on a conceptual study. Their design called for a building that measured 239 by 76 meters (784 by

Left: As a small boy, in 1909, Paul Edward Garber (1899–1992) watched Orville Wright demonstrate his military aircraft near Washington, D.C., and he learned about kites from Alexander Graham Bell. At 15, he owned his first full-scale biplane glider. World War I ended as Garber began his flight training. For 72 years, this aviation enthusiast played a major role in preserving aeronautical history as a member of the Smithsonian Institution's staff, first as a model maker and exhibit preparator in 1920 and then as the primary collector and savior of aircraft and related artifacts, taking some time off as a Naval officer during World War II. Garber created the Silver Hill Facility in Suitland, Md., in the early 1950s to house the National Air Museum's growing collections. After the National Air and Space Museum opened in 1976, the Smithsonian improved conditions at the storage facility, opening some of its buildings for public tours and planning further improvements to safeguard the collections. In 1980, the off-site facility was renamed the Paul E. Garber Preservation, Restoration, and Storage Facility to honor this influential pioneer. But Paul called it "Garber's Harbor."

Below: There was not enough room at Silver Hill for all the World War II aircraft that Paul Garber moved from Illinois in the early 1950s. By the 1980s, the complex was covered with metal buildings, all full of aircraft and spacecraft parts and pieces, but conditions there were not conducive to saving aviation history.

No-frills tours at the Garber Facility, led by volunteer docents, were popular among aviation enthusiasts.

250 ft), with a height of 30 meters (97 ft). The cost was estimated at $40 million in 1964. In a 1965 report, Museum Director S. Paul Johnston was reminded by his advisors that once the building was in place "its dimensions and its physical capacity are fixed for all foreseeable time." The building would have to accommodate a flexible exhibit program to remain viable.[3]

With the United States and the Soviet Union waging a space race, visitors to the Air Museum in its temporary quarters on the Mall got their first glimpse of the spacecraft that took American astronauts to this new regime of flight. Nearly 2 million people visited the displays, taking in the technology and the magic. In 1966, the Museum's name was expanded to reflect this new area of collecting. But construction of what was now the National Air and Space Museum (NASM), while approved, was thwarted by what was described as the "Viet Nam problem." For the immediate future, there was no Federal funding available for new museums, with an expensive war to wage in Southeast Asia.

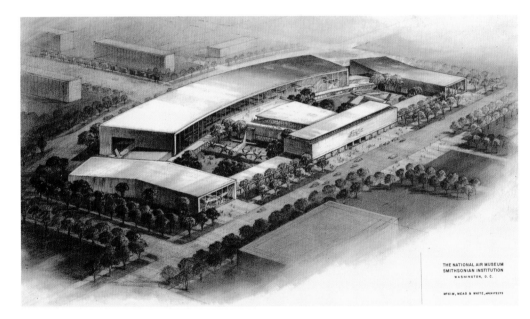

THE NATIONAL AIR MUSEUM
SMITHSONIAN INSTITUTION
WASHINGTON, D. C.

McKIM, MEAD & WHITE, ARCHITECTS

Left: McKim, Mead, and White of New York designed a crescent-shaped building for the museum in the mid-1950s. The site for this design, in downtown Washington, was used instead for a shopping complex, as part of a larger plan to redevelop the southwestern part of the city.

Below: Hellmuth, Obata + Kassabaum of St. Louis was awarded a contract to design a museum for the three-city-block site on the National Mall finally approved for the National Air and Space Museum. HOK's rectangular design was unveiled in 1964. The architects envisioned a building 239 by 76 meters (784 by 250 ft), with glass walls and elevated viewing opportunities.

In 1970, Senator Barry Goldwater forcefully brought to his colleagues' attention the poor condition of the national collection of aircraft and space artifacts in substandard housing at Silver Hill. And he pointed out that the Air and Space Museum was receiving only 2 percent of the Institution's budget but attracting 15 percent of its visitors. Approval for the new building and construction funding was made available the next year, but with the passage of so many years since the design team completed their construction drawings, the $40 million building was now estimated at $60–70 million. As the architects set about redesigning the project to meet budget, they learned that they had a firm opening date— July 4, 1976. In September 1972, earthmoving equipment started transforming a parking lot into a construction site in downtown Washington.

Museum staff began moving aircraft and exhibitry into the 23 galleries of the new pink Tennessee marble and glass structure in late 1975. President Gerald Ford opened the National Air and Space Museum on July 1, 1976. One million visitors passed through the doors during the first month, 10 million during the first year.

In 1976, as the Museum opened, the collection numbered approximately 23,000 objects, of which about 10 to 15 percent were on display. The Museum's team from the Silver Hill Facility in Suitland had relocated objects from the "temporary" metal building on the Mall, from the Arts and Industries Building (formerly the home of the National Museum), from the storage and restoration facility in Maryland, and from numerous other locations around the country. But the warehouses and back lots of Silver Hill were far from empty. The first order of business in Suitland was to get aircraft that had long been stored outdoors moved inside the metal buildings to better protect them.

Below: Aircraft and spacecraft could be seen on display at the Arts and Industries Building in 1969.

Bottom: Conditions at Silver Hill were crowded and were not ideal for preserving the collection "in perpetuity."

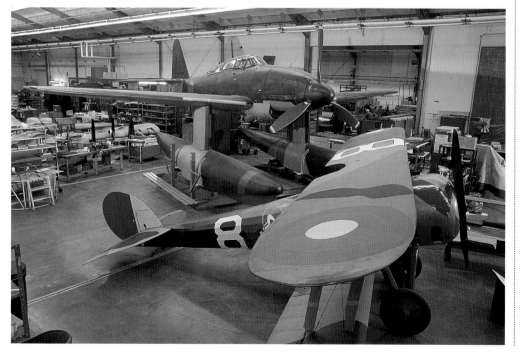

Curator Lou Casey and Paul Garber receive the B-8M gyrocopter for the collection from Igor Bensen in 1973, while a line-up of rockets and missiles stand sentry at the Arts and Industries Building.

Above left: Construction of the National Air and Space Museum started in the fall of 1972. Dimensions: 193.5 meters (635 ft) long, 68.6 meters (225 ft) wide, 25.3 meters (83 ft) high.

Above right: The new Museum was an immediate success when it opened in July 1976, earning the title "most visited museum in the world," with 10 million people visiting during the first year.

Right: Museum staff and contractors hang a DC-3 in Eastern Air Lines livery at the National Air and Space Museum.

Secondly, the Museum needed to better account for what it owned, and the staff began a massive inventory project. And all the while, curators continued to collect. The Museum's mission was to "memorialize" the history of aviation and spaceflight, in large part by collecting, caring for, and displaying objects that reflected that history. But at the Museum on the Mall, where the exhibit galleries were filling up, the largest aircraft on display was the Douglas DC-3, hanging in the Air Transportation Gallery. With a wingspan of 29 meters (95 ft) and length of 20 metres (64.5 ft), this commercial airliner was developed in the 1930s. In Space Hall, the Skylab orbital workshop reigned. Astronauts called Skylab home in the early 1970s. Where would the Air and Space Museum exhibit modern aircraft and spacecraft, especially large bombers, airliners, and cargo aircraft and the next generation of reusable spacecraft? Where could the Museum better care for the many objects still in storage at Silver Hill? Where was there more room for a growing collection?

Finding a Site for an "Annex"

In the 1960s, when the Air Museum was searching for a permanent home, proponents of aviation in the Commonwealth of Virginia had tried to tempt the Smithsonian to build its museum at the newly constructed Dulles Airport in northern Virginia or at least display some of its stored aircraft in the terminal. In a reply to one of the supporters of the Dulles site in 1966, Louis S. Casey, curator of aircraft, explained that a Smithsonian museum "rarely has more than 5–10 percent of specimens on exhibit," with the bulk of its collection in the "study" category. And the Museum was hopeful that Congress would soon approve funding for the design and construction of an appropriately sized building for the growing collections.[4] But the persistent Virginians suggested in 1967 that, after the new museum was built, the Smithsonian could relocate its Silver Hill Facility to Dulles or nearby, and the private citizens sought the leverage of the Division of Aeronautics of the State Corporation Commission.[5] The Commission's Director thought the idea excellent: "I am sure it will attract many additional tourists, general aviation pilots and business executives who are interested in aviation and recognize its contribution to everyone's economic well being."[6] When the Virginians' letter-writing campaign reached the Administrator of the Federal Aviation Administration (FAA) and the Aircraft Owners and Pilots Association, the Smithsonian asked them to temper their enthusiasm.[7] And the FAA Director of the Bureau of National Capital Airports

advised all parties that an air museum "is not only inconsistent with the Master Plan for ultimate development of the Airport, but more significantly, would not be compatible with the operation of Dulles as a commercial airport complex which many consider will one day be the world's finest."[8]

Discussions about a Dulles site and delays in Congressional funding for the building that would house the "inspirational collection" prompted curator Casey in 1969 to suggest that NASM use private funding to construct a multi-building complex at the northern boundary of the airport for a minimum of 50 aircraft. In a memorandum to the head of the National Museum, Casey wrote that this "active study" collection could be made available to the public and researchers; would relieve storage pressure; would "place the specimens in their natural habitat, an active airport"; and fit the model being used by other aviation museums.[9] That same year, another NASM staff member was told about a 376.5-hectare (930-acre) site west of the airport that would be a "near perfect spot" for the Museum.[10]

Through the early 1970s, various citizen and Commonwealth organizations continued to resurrect the idea of the Smithsonian coming to the Dulles region, without success. The managers of the National Air and Space Museum were necessarily focused on their immediate task of winning support for a building in Washington, D.C.

Aircraft flying high in the Air Transportation Gallery at NASM. The DC-3, which represents 1930s technology, is the largest aircraft installed at the Museum on the Mall.

In the minutes of an April 1971 meeting of the Dulles International Airport Development Commission, it was reported that there was now some considerable enthusiasm by the Smithsonian for moving their historical aircraft storage facility to Dulles but this enthusiasm was not shared by the FAA. The report goes on to say that the objections "were based on a fear that a gift of land to the Smithsonian Institute [*sic*] would set a dangerous precedent and that having a division of the Smithsonian at the airport might well cause crowds (not otherwise utilizing the facilities) to flock to the airport thus congesting the approaches to the airport to the detriment of passenger service…."[11] And a plan for the Smithsonian to use the site of a transportation exposition near Dulles in 1972, offered as a joint resolution of the Virginia Airports Authority, the Virginia Advisory Committee on Aviation, and the Development Commission, was turned down by the Institution.

NASM Director Michael Collins, in 1974, with the new Museum under construction, raised some prescient questions with the Commonwealth's Advisory Committee on Aviation. He asked if Virginia was going to make a formal proposal for the Smithsonian to relocate its storage facility near Dulles. "What land? Who owns it? What buildings? What money—state, federal, or private? Is legislation required? How about a feasibility study? Who will pay for that? Why Dulles rather than some other place?"[12] In the years to come, these questions would be asked repeatedly.

Not long after the National Air and Space Museum opened in the summer of 1976, Don Lopez, head of the Aeronautics Department, discussed the future of aircraft acquisition and storage with Director Collins. Looking for a long-term solution, Lopez thought that it was essential to find or build a "large industrial type storage facility … at an airport location." He mentioned Dulles or Andrews Air Force Base as two possible locations in the region. He went on to suggest that the facility should be able to accommodate aircraft as large as a Boeing 747, because they will eventually "become Museum pieces, just as the current crop of large military aircraft will." If the Air Force could be persuaded to dedicate hangars and ramp space to NASM, Lopez favored the Andrews option. It was close by, secure, accessible, and, if donated, economical. Any military base, however, was subject to restrictions during an emergency, and a civilian operation, like a museum, would be cut easily if the base needed programmatic elbow room. Dulles was more distant but had the advantage of being "an automatic tourist center. It is easy to conceive of free tour buses from the terminal to the satellite museum," he wrote. But at Dulles, NASM would have to build hangars. The World War II

fighter ace did not recommend relocating the reserve collection to a remote city, such as Pensacola or Wichita. Such a move would require a "drastic reshaping of current policy, administration, manpower and so on." And it was not viable for the Museum to simply stop acquiring objects. This was a "dead-end" approach.[13]

In 1980, NASM Deputy Director Melvin R. Zisfein and Assistant Director for Aeronautics Lopez completed a survey of all the major airports in the Washington area to determine which would be suitable for an annex. Winning candidates had to be within one hour's drive of NASM; the annex could not interfere with the basic mission of the airport; the airfield had to be active and able to receive large jet aircraft; there had to be sufficient room for expansion; and the project needed the support of airport and local officials. Of the six they examined, Dulles was just right; Baltimore-Washington Airport came in second, but officials in Maryland were not interested in the idea. Optional features for this annex included an IMAX® theater, a center for visiting researchers, a simulated control tower, "participatory" exhibits, and a telescope platform.[14] By late 1983, the Smithsonian's Board of Regents had endorsed an annex at Dulles, and the FAA had set aside some 40.5 hectares (100 acres) for this purpose. Authorization bills were introduced in Congress. The grand total price for a four-building complex was $66.7 million, and if the feasibility study could begin in mid-1985, the Museum hoped that the first phase of the "second best air and space museum in the world" could be completed by 1990.[15]

In the Milestones of Flight Gallery at NASM, future astronaut candidates take a close look at Gemini 4.

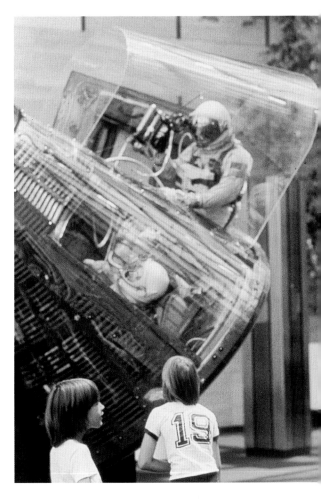

24

CHAPTER TWO

Planning and Designing the "Dulles Extension"

THE NATIONAL AIR AND SPACE MUSEUM (NASM) ON THE MALL OPENED ITS DOORS SOME 30 YEARS AFTER CONGRESS DIRECTED THE SMITHSONIAN TO ESTABLISH THE INSTITUTION'S AIR WING IN 1946. PLANNING, DESIGNING, AND BUILDING THE MUSEUM'S SECOND PERMANENT PUBLIC FACILITY WOULD TAKE NEARLY THAT LONG. SERIOUS INTEREST IN DULLES AS THE SITE FOR AN EXTENSION WAS DECLARED BY MUSEUM STAFF IN 1977, BUT THE NEW BUILDING WOULD NOT OPEN AT THE NORTHERN VIRGINIA AIRPORT FOR ANOTHER 26 YEARS. THE ARCHITECTS' WORK— PLANNING AND LOCATING A SITE AND DESIGNING THE STRUCTURE—WAS ONLY HALF THE STORY DURING THE 1980S AND '90S. THE HARDER BATTLE WAS SECURING CONGRESSIONAL APPROVAL AND FUNDING TO PURSUE THAT DESIGN.

Supporters of the Museum enthusiastically predicted that the Dulles Wing would open in 1988. Aircraft listed as candidates for indoor shelter included the prototype of the Boeing 707, the Boeing Stratoliner, a B-25, a B-17, and an F-4. A 5,400-square-meter (60,000-sq-ft) restoration hangar was part of the concept.

Aviation and space artist Robert T. McCall provided this concept drawing of the "Dulles Wing" at the request of NASM Director Walter J. Boyne in 1984. Used with permission from the artist.

Site Selection and Congressional Approval

IN SEPTEMBER 1983, the Smithsonian's governing body, the Board of Regents, agreed that the Institution should proceed with formal planning for a second National Air and Space Museum facility, to be built at Dulles International Airport. Doug Wonderlic of the Smithsonian's Office of Design and Construction initiated the task by writing a scope of work for a study "to determine the feasibility and requirements for developing a NASM wing at Dulles." Such a study would typically be performed in two phases: development of program and facility requirements, along with a site selection study, a transportation study, and a preliminary cost estimate; this would be followed by a comprehensive master plan.[1] Concurrent with the Smithsonian's efforts, Dulles was also finalizing its updated master plan of the airport property.

The first concept for the Dulles complex included four hangars, 76 by 91 meters (250 by 300 ft) each. One would serve as a restoration shop, while the others would house aircraft and spacecraft on public display and in storage. Don Lopez recalled that he was asked to draw a picture of what the Museum needed at Dulles, and, since he could draw rectangles pretty good, that's what he did. An exhibits designer colored them in, and the first visualization of the annex was created.

In the airport master plan, largely undeveloped buffer zones provided generous clearances between the runways and the airport's boundaries, including perimeter areas that were to remain park-like. These areas would provide a visual and acoustical buffer for the benefit of the surrounding community. However, some limited development would be allowed if it were consistent with adjacent off-airport development. Airport planners determined that NASM's proposed museum was compatible with the recommended land use in the buffer area, and nine sites were identified by the Federal Aviation Administration (FAA), which owned Washington Dulles, for further study.[2]

A unique band of Dulles area citizens, business people, and government officials formed a partnership in 1985. The Air and Space Heritage Council— established by the Washington Dulles Task Force, the Aero Club of Washington, and the National Aviation Club—proposed a privately funded national home for the space shuttle *Enterprise,* which was scheduled for delivery to Dulles by the National Aeronautics and Space Administration (NASA) in November 1985 for transfer to NASM. The Museum's storage problems would be multiplied several times when it accepted the prototype shuttle orbiter. This craft was too large to take to any urban location, and a new home at the airport would be ideal. Senior managers at the Smithsonian hoped that the highly publicized arrival of the shuttle flying in on the back of a Boeing 747 would energize Congress and hasten approval and funding for the planning and design of the Dulles annex. Authorization bills were sponsored, but they did not move far down the approval pipeline.[3]

Air and Space Heritage Council members volunteered to fund the feasibility study for the project as an act of faith. They believed that the new museum would be economically important to the region,

help promote aviation and the airport, and provide an incomparable educational resource. Led by Carrington Williams, Leo J. Schefer, and Thomas G. Morr, this group of community supporters kept true to its vision for the next 18 years: "The museum is expected to appeal to a broad segment of American aviation and space interests, as well as focusing national and international interest in the Dulles area of the Nation's Capital and Virginia." They expected between 750,000 and 1 million visitors during the first year of operation. The Council's first act to expedite construction of the new museum was to sponsor a version of the feasibility study called for by the Smithsonian in 1983.[4] As engineers and architects began their investigation, the private supporters of the project calculated revenue streams and discussed various mechanisms for private financing.

As part of the feasibility study, Deputy Director Don Lopez led an eight-person team from the Air and Space Museum, which set to work defining in greater detail what was needed at the annex.[5] On the team were staff from the Garber Facility, exhibit designers, and curators. The nine-week study was accomplished by Dewberry & Davis Engineers, Architects, Planners, and Surveyors. The planners recommended a phased approach to building the facility, with the first 6,480-square-meter (72,000-sq-ft) building being dedicated to the space shuttle, with an IMAX® theater for revenue generation and a 500-car parking lot. Dewberry & Davis' report tackled site selection, master planning, engineering, programming, and conceptual design and provided a cost estimate. The NASM team defined its first criteria for floor loading, hangar door dimensions, temperature and humidity controls, light levels, and security.

The ideal site for the annex at the airport would be accessible to visitors and arriving aircraft; it would not impact airport operations; it would be economical to develop; and there had to be room for future growth. Four western sites were easily eliminated because of their proximity to existing or proposed runways. Two northern sites offered little room for expansion and were close to operational areas. Two eastern sites adjacent to Route 28 and a southern location near the intersection of Routes 28 and 50 were considered to have the most potential. Planners unanimously chose the 73-hectare (180-acre) southern site as the best positioned land for an aerospace museum.[6]

Dewberry and Davis' concept featured a long-span steel-truss shuttle building, which would be joined by additional buildings as funding became available to form a Dulles Wing of the National Air and Space Museum. The cluster of rectangular buildings would be located on the northern half of the site, which was bisected by an east-west running stream, Cain's Branch. Engineers described transportation and utility improvements that were slated for the area, declaring them adequate for a public facility that would attract large numbers of visitors.

Visitors to phase one of the Dulles wing would first catch sight of *Enterprise* from a second-level vantage point: "Upon arrival on the second level, the visitor

proceeds directly to the exhibit hall entrance as the view of the shuttle unfolds dramatically at the front of the spacecraft."[7] And the roof would be capable of supporting artifacts suspended from the structure. The 500-seat theater would function as a separate but connected attraction. Estimators predicted the cost at a little over $7 million, but Museum officials increased that estimate to $12 million a few months later to better account for the cost of

The southernmost site evaluated by the site team promised the Museum the best access and the most land at Washington Dulles. NASM's new facility would be 6.4 kilometers (4 miles) south of the main terminal. The airport opened in 1962 on 4,049 hectares (10,000 acres), enough land to establish a buffer zone separating airport operations from residential and commercial properties. Dulles serves nearly 20 million passengers a year and is adding runways and passenger amenities.

Visitors would view the space shuttle from two levels. Satellites and aircraft would be suspended overhead. Senator Barry Goldwater was especially vocal about the importance of making the shuttle available to the public: "Aerospace sciences are a cutting edge for the technological developments upon which the health of our economy and our exports, as well as the living standards of the American people, depend. That is why the timely expansion of the National Air and Space Museum is important—it helps to bridge the education gap and it inspires the young who will have to face the challenges and problems of our expanding technical knowledge in the future."

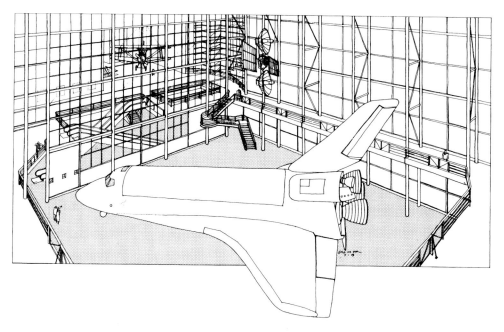

A private developer proposed a "National Space Park" that would feature *Enterprise* on property near Dulles in an amusement park-like setting.

NASA delivered the space shuttle *Enterprise* to Washington Dulles in late November 1985 and transferred ownership to NASM in early December at a gala held in a hangar at the airport. The evening event was emceed by William Shatner, Captain James Kirk of that other famous but fictional spacecraft of the same name. *Enterprise,* the first shuttle orbiter, manufactured in 1976, was used to fit-check the launch pads and to verify the approach and landing performance of the spacecraft.

infrastructure and move-in. The rest of the wing would cost $87.4 million, the Museum predicted in February 1986, an estimate that would increase to $100 million before the end of the next year.[8] To get this work started, the Secretary of the Smithsonian requested $1 million at an August 1986 hearing before the Senate Committee on Rules and Administration, but Congressional priorities did not yet include a new museum. Officials at FAA, however, did approve of the Dulles concept and executed an option in September 1986 to lease land to the Smithsonian for its future expansion.

With no Congressional funding in sight for a Dulles facility, in the spring of 1988 the Smithsonian elected to use internal planning monies to move the staff's concept work to the next level. The Office of Design and Construction contracted with Skidmore, Owings & Merrill (SOM) for a 16-week planning study that would formalize the Air and Space Museum's objectives and requirements. Working with staff, the contractors would define the new facility's purpose and give it thematic identity, list its components, and explain the facility's programmatic relationships to other Smithsonian assets. Dulles corridor backers of the project objected that there had been studies enough; it was time for Congressional action and time to lobby Commonwealth of Virginia lawmakers for their fiscal

Large cranes were used to de-mate the 68,040-kilogram (150,000-lb) shuttle from the Boeing 747 after NASA delivered it to Dulles in 1985.

To protect *Enterprise* from the elements, NASM built a temporary storage hangar at Dulles for the shuttle and other large artifacts that needed shelter until the new museum wing could be built.

support of this new tourist destination.[9] NASM Director Martin O. Harwit argued the case for more methodical planning work while the Museum's friends in Congress garnered the necessary support to approve the project, but he agreed with Air and Space Heritage Council members that the time had come to give Virginia the opportunity to assist the Smithsonian.

The SOM team, at the direction of the Smithsonian, opened the door to more expansive thinking about what was possible at Dulles. At Director Harwit's urging, dozens of Smithsonian staff were interviewed, and new ideas for programs "off-campus" bubbled to the surface. By late summer, the official purpose had been defined. At Dulles, NASM would expand its collections, augment all of its existing functions, and develop and test new exhibit concepts. "It will be literally an extension of the Mall Museum, and not an independent museum in its own

right," wrote Harwit's team. The primary function would still be to receive and display large aircraft and spacecraft and preserve and restore the collection under stable environmental conditions. But at Dulles, the Museum would also present "exhibits on the impact of human activity on global environmental systems" and make available interdisciplinary and interactive exhibits on the principles of aeronautics, rocketry, and global environmental systems. A theater, solar observatory, research facilities, and conference center were suggested as longer-range additions.[10] But not all the thinking was so expansive.

The collection team at Garber and many of the curators limited their focus to the needs of the artifacts and archival collections that required a better home to ensure their survival and accessibility, and they thought in terms of functional requirements. By fall, SOM had estimated the footprint needed to meet

NASM's first set of priorities for the extension, to include exhibit hangars and galleries, a restoration hangar and collections storage unit, classrooms and theaters, archives, research facilities, and visitor accommodations. SOM recommended 73,800 square meters (820,000 sq ft) and estimated the cost at $201.79 million, including site work.[11] And even with all the new ideas for what could be accomplished at Dulles, the severe shortage of space for the exhibition of artifacts, especially large aircraft and spacecraft, topped all the lists of reasons for the extension.

Among the senior managers at the Smithsonian, there was no forged unity of support for NASM's expanded programs at Dulles. One key person wrote that the SOM report read more like a "prospectus for buying swampland in Florida, rather than a document which provides a vision for the future." The budget director could not find enough compelling reasons why NASM should proceed with its expansion. And another senior staffer apologized to the Secretary of the Smithsonian for the failure of the "miserable report" from SOM. She observed that the problem stemmed from "the tension between the primacy of NASM's needs and the opportunity to create something broader in concept."[12] Secretary Robert Mc. Adams, however, supported the findings of the report, with some minor changes, and forwarded copies to the Board of Regents. In his critique, Adams offered the following rationale: "The reason NASM is so popular, and ranks so high in the Smithsonian's own ordering of its priorities, is because of the centrality of the achievements it portrays...." He declared that these achievements are

"unambiguously ours." "With any sense of history at all, our successors will always want to preserve and celebrate this. We owe it to the Smithsonian's mission to set aside permanently the means by which they can do so."[13] All it would take, he told the Regents, was 81 hectares (200 acres) of land and $300 million.

While the Smithsonian was planning for the future at Dulles, Air and Space Heritage Council members were knocking on doors in Richmond, Virginia, generating interest and enthusiasm for the new venture.

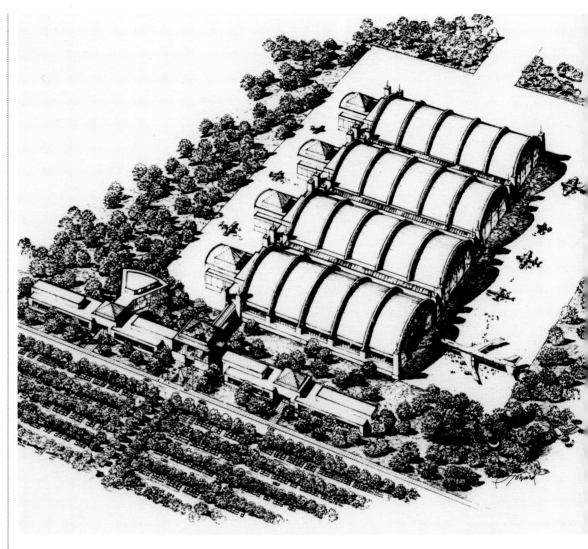

Four hangars capped by four exhibit galleries were featured in the conceptual design produced by Skidmore, Owings & Merrill for the National Air and Space Museum's Dulles facility in 1988.

Visitors to Dulles would also be able to observe artifact restoration, as illustrated in the architects' 1988 study.

Airport (BWI). And, yes, Maryland could provide financial incentives, too.[14]

Given political realities, the Smithsonian was obliged to take seriously the offer from Maryland, and contracted with Hellmuth, Obata + Kassabaum (HOK), the architects who had designed the Air and Space Museum on the Mall, to conduct a detailed comparison of BWI and Dulles. HOK had won a competition to prepare a site evaluation study and master plan for the Dulles project in early 1989, which had been authorized and funded as part of the Smithsonian's Federal budget. The first step was a thorough understanding of what the Museum required of a site. In the spring of 1989, site evaluation goals and criteria were established to create standards for comparing the two locations. Listening to the long-range goals of the Museum, HOK concluded that the site needed to accommodate a 135,000-square-meter (1.5 million-square-foot) facility for all the amenities and potential described in the Skidmore, Owings & Merrill report. By year's end, both sites had been thoroughly scrutinized and judged according to 11 criteria. HOK concluded that both sites were viable locations. At Dulles, there was more land available for long-term expansion, but when considering access, ecosystem impacts, availability of utilities, location, and compatibility with surrounding land use, the architects found few differences.[15] The financial incentives offered by both states were also comparable. Secretary Adams asked the Board of Regents to confirm the Institution's intent to plan and build a second facility, pending Congressional approval, at Washington Dulles, the international gateway to the Nation's capital. They did so in January

Tom Morr was an enthusiastic but low-profile advocate for the Museum among elected officials and staff alike. The case he made was simple: millions of visitors will find their way to the new museum at Dulles, leaving behind money well spent at Virginia hotels, restaurants, and gas stations. An investment in the infrastructure required for the new facility would be more than paid for by future tax revenues. Add to that the educational resources that would be made available at Dulles to students of the Commonwealth. But as Morr and Harwit were moving forward with plans for a partnership with Virginia, the governor of Maryland suggested that the Smithsonian build its new facility at Baltimore Washington International

1990, and Smithsonian officials renewed their conversations with officials in Virginia on potential financial support. Gratefully, collections experts at NASM quit trying to figure out how to move the space shuttle from Virginia to Maryland and prepared to receive another spectacular, large artifact at Dulles, the SR-71 reconnaissance aircraft.

The Office of Design and Construction and NASM kicked off the master planning exercise with HOK in June 1990 while Congress was entertaining bills to approve the extension. Senators Garn, Moynihan, Warner, and Robb sponsored the Senate bill in May 1990, with the companion bill being introduced in the House by Representatives Conte, Mineta, and Whitten in June. Virginia's offer of support from Governor Douglas Wilder in April had outlined a package valued at $40 million, as well as an interest-free loan and bonding authority. Congress was advised that the first phase of the project could be built for about $162 million, with total build-out estimated at $330 million. Phase 1 would include most of the fundamental infrastructure required for the entire project as well as exhibition hangar space, a restoration hangar, one exhibition gallery, collections storage space, archives, offices, theater, and other visitor services amenities. Two additional phases of the 135,000-square-meter (1.5 million-sq-ft) dream would incorporate additional hangars and three more galleries.[16]

Museum teams formed to consider carefully all aspects of the new facility. Curators debated over what artifacts should be installed and in what order. Collections care staff deliberated over how to relocate aircraft and spacecraft to Virginia. Both groups pondered the condition of collections that had been in

The U.S. Air Force transferred ownership of SR-71 64-17972 to the National Air and Space Museum after flying it to Dulles on March 6, 1990. Lt. Col. Ed Yielding and Lt. Col. Joseph Vida flew the aircraft coast to coast in 64 minutes, with an average speed of 3,418 km/h (2,124 mph), a record. SR-71s were used for high-flying military reconnaissance missions from the late 1960s until the mid-1990s.

storage for decades. Educators and visitor services staff weighed in on their specific needs. And physical plant experts reviewed approaches to maintaining a stable environment for the protection of the collections in what promised to be a huge facility.

In the midst of this teamwork, the Museum was informed that public officials in Colorado had proposed that the Smithsonian use Stapleton Airport in Denver as the site of the new museum and promised the Federal government significant savings in the process. A new international airport was under construction near Denver, and Stapleton was ripe for redevelopment. The offer was delivered via Colorado Congressman David Skaggs. With the promise of savings hanging in the air, Congress asked the Smithsonian to take this offer seriously. After months of exchanging information, a small delegation from NASM traveled to Denver in late 1990 and spent several days crawling through baggage handling areas, examining chillers and boilers, measuring spaces, and talking with local officials. With HOK's help, the Museum made the case that establishing the extension so far from Washington, with the attendant costs of relocating the objects and building a duplicate staff for the western site, would actually cost more in the long run.

Over the next several months, offers from all over the country poured in for the Institution's consideration. Cities with military installations that were being downsized or with airports that were underutilized wrote to their members of Congress suggesting that they had a deal for the Smithsonian. NASM lost months of valuable planning time as they carefully considered these offers, but no bargains were found and no acceptable plan for how to divide the collection and move it to a distant facility was agreed upon by staff. Meanwhile, new bills authorizing the extension died in committee during another session of Congress.

The scrutiny of so many members of Congress, as well as the Government Accounting Office, which examined the site selection process, forced the Museum to focus on what were truly its most important priorities as it planned the new facility. With cost estimates increasing with each fine-tuning of the design and with questions being asked by lawmakers representing states distant from Virginia, Martin Harwit directed his team to tighten its belt. He wrote that after all the various groups within the Museum had expressed their wishes for the new facility it was clear that those "wishes reflect a range of different assumptions, which certainly can be defended individually, but do not add up to a program that the Museum as a whole can propose to Congress." He outlined two global assumptions within which the Museum must work. First, the overall cost must be kept to $330 million, with the first phase being kept to $162. And secondly, the first phase would serve two primary purposes: to provide better care for the artifacts and permit exhibition of large objects in a way that features their purposes, significance, and social impact. He wrote that the exhibitions "must be clearly thematic, rather than encyclopedic." And the extension would not be a palace; the design would fit the character of the airport and provide the Museum with solutions to its most immediate needs.

Opposite: NASM stored the SR-71 outside at Dulles until MIC Industries, in partnership with other contractors, donated a pre-engineered building for its protection.

Walter Urbanek, Project Manager, Hellmuth, Obata + Kassabaum

At the opening gala, which was a black tie affair, my wife asked me how I felt now that the museum was opening to the public. I told her that it felt like being at our daughter's graduation. As parents, you were there from her beginning, you watched when she took her first steps, you prepared her for life as best you could, but now she's no longer your responsibility and you trust she can make it on her own.

When I visit the Hazy Center, I remember all the people that helped design and build it. Many of the designers are no longer with HOK; two of them have died, but I know what each of them contributed. This project went through three NASM Directors and I know how each of their visions helped the project. I especially remember those core people who stuck it out through the entire process, which for me began in 1989. I also find myself looking at all the visitors, especially the veterans like my father and can appreciate the delight in their eyes.

Staffing levels would be kept to a minimum. Collections would be staged and moved over several years. And the Museum would find it difficult to launch major new exhibitions and other programs at the Museum downtown when energies were required for Dulles.[17]

Despite the Museum's dedication to a tighter focus on its core mission and insistence that Dulles was the best site for its new facility, members of Congress continued to debate the issue of site selection well into 1992, with elected officials from Virginia, Colorado, and Maryland being the most vocal. The Institution was advised not to conduct any site-specific planning during its work with the architects, putting on hold the master planning exercise initiated with HOK. In its report on the Smithsonian's fiscal year 1992 funding request, the House Interior Appropriations Subcommittee recommended that the site selection process should be opened to national competition if the extension's scope included anything more than storage and restoration functions. Museum staff scrambled to downsize the program further, reducing the complex to 60,300 square meters (670,000 sq ft) and scaling back the public programs. The project cost was billed at $162 million with operating expenses estimated at $10 million annually. Mention of subsequent phases was dropped. The Institution feared that an open competition could cost $5 million to conduct, at a time when no monies had yet been authorized for design. Museum officials offered to develop a funding strategy aimed at minimizing the required level of Federal funding needed for construction through major contributions from private sector sources.[18]

Bills were offered, debated, rejected, or left to linger on Capitol Hill in 1992. Senators and Representatives who supported the Smithsonian's efforts were persistent, however, and in February 1993 Representatives Mineta, McDade, and Natcher introduced House bill H.R.847 to authorize the Smithsonian to plan and design the National Air and Space Museum extension at Dulles, with an appropriation of $8 million for that work. Senators Warner, Moynihan, and Sasser sponsored Senate bill S.535 with the same terms. On August 2, President Bill Clinton signed public law 103-57 making it official.[19]

As the Museum's staff renewed its work with HOK to design the Dulles facility, senior managers at the Institution struggled over descriptions and strategies that struck the proper balance for a facility that would be designed to meet NASM's most immediate needs for the collection but could still be lauded as a significant addition to the Institution that would serve as a major facility for many decades. By the fall of 1993, the building was being described as an "architecturally aesthetic hangar," and the program included displays of over-sized artifacts, state-of-the-art restoration and storage, a large-screen theater and museum shop to generate revenue, and spaces solely dedicated to education and other related outreach activities.[20] And as the year closed, Smithsonian officials realized that their chances for securing Federal dollars for construction after the design was finished were slim. NASM pledged to use its private-side trust funds to conduct a fundraising feasibility study and market research.

Design

HOK's contract with the Smithsonian for master planning included an option for design services. NASM's core team of collections staff, curators, and designers had developed a close working relationship with project manager Walter Urbanek and the architects at HOK, and the Museum recommended no further competition as planning work blurred into design tasks during the mid-1990s. Exactly what did the Museum need and just who would come to this new extension? The design team spent several years answering these two questions as they moved the design from concept to schematic design to design development to actual construction drawings.

Smithsonian planner Doug Wonderlic continued his steady and meticulous guidance of HOK's work for the Smithsonian. At NASM, many of the technical answers to questions about the needs of the collection came to Al Bachmeier of the Garber Facility, who had helped plan the move into the Museum on the Mall. Lin Ezell, Assistant Director for Collections Management, was charged with coordinating details among the many departments with an interest in Dulles. Curators examined their collections to assess their most immediate needs and, with designers, group them into display settings that could tell stories. Space planning started with a conceptual identification of the Museum's activities at the new facility. Architects called this exercise "programming." It was difficult for many on the team to back away from the specific requirements of door widths and concrete thicknesses and think in the abstract, guided by facilitators who didn't know a biplane from a jet. But the exercise was invaluable. As a result, HOK was able to chart the Museum's requirements and adjacencies. They knew what the conservator needed and whom he needed to interact with most. They came to understand how visitors and educators would interact and where that activity should take place. In charts, planners at HOK translated program needs into physical spaces and subdivided those into individual workshops, classrooms, hangars, and offices, each with a defined space requirement. They diagrammed the routes of travel of people and objects among the areas of the conceptual building. HOK was drawing circles and squares and connecting them with arrows and dots. For some of the NASM team, it seemed like taking one step back after seeing the hangar drawings of the late 1980s. Midway through this work in 1992/93, the belt-tightening prompted by Congress took place, and the team stopped work, regrouped, and recalculated.[21]

With construction costs already an issue, NASM asked HOK to conduct engineering studies of several building shapes. What style of building would give the Museum the most space for the least dollars? Since there was plenty of land at Dulles to build on, would it be smarter to build a large but low building, or would a more traditional arched hangar with space and strength

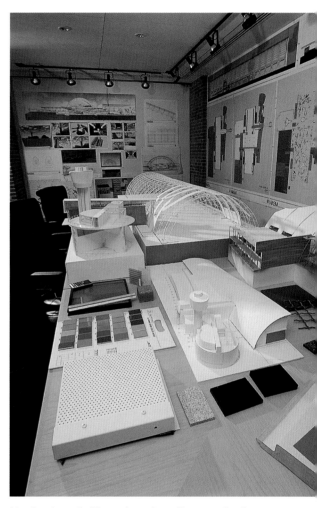

After listening to the Museum's needs, architects translated those requirements into specific spaces, always keeping in mind that the new facility would be located at a busy international airport.

Top: Consultants on the environmental assessment team identified 62 species of animals and 332 plant species on the forested tract of land set aside for the Dulles extension. Between the 18th century and the early 20th, farmers had planted row crops and grazed livestock on this land. When airport managers acquired the land in the 1950s, they had the fields planted over in pines. No rare or endangered plants or animals were discovered.

Above: Archeologists searched the proposed building area for evidence of historic structures and artifacts as part of the environmental assessment. At four locations they found objects that prompted more thorough excavations, but none of the findings was considered historically significant. The field team dug about 1,300 shovel test pits, finding some brick, porcelain, and stoneware fragments, nails, oyster shells, and glass. Along Cain's Branch stream, digs produced waste chips from making stone tools, projectile point fragments, two stone scrapers, and rocks cracked from fires, all evidence that early Native Americans had hunted and frequented the area. Cain's Branch would be left undisturbed.

to hang artifacts be more economical? In 1989, the Museum had been thinking in terms of buildings with open spans of 110 meters (360 ft). Was this approach, with its high cost, still viable? Engineers from Spiegel Zamecnik & Shah learned about the weights and wingspans of aircraft in the collection, and they introduced Museum staff to the principles of structural engineering.

HOK's engineers evaluated conventional systems that are custom designed but made from standard materials, as well as proprietary systems marketed as a manufactured system of components under a trade name. In a 1995 report, HOK reported on nine conventional systems of trusses, long-span joists, and arches and nine trademarked building systems. Open spans ranged from 35 meters to 125 meters (115–410 ft). But the engineers did not confine their comparisons to structural members; they compared substructures, columns, bracing, roof decks and roofing, and the exterior closures of each building type. HOK's conclusion: for spans in the 65 to 100-meter (213–328-ft) range, conventional truss frame construction was the most economical; for spans over 100 meters (328 ft), the curved arch could be built for a slightly better price. When the architects factored in the groupings and sizes of aircraft and spacecraft, they recommended that NASM consider a structure with height and strength enough to hang many of its artifacts, making use of the volume of the building, not just its ground-level footprint. During the concept design phase, the team would use this data to evaluate several building shapes and sizes.[22]

Another part of the HOK team was literally in the field during the early and mid-1990s examining the site at Dulles. Wetlands were precisely located and mapped. Flora and fauna were identified. Archeological surveys and digs were conducted. Noise levels were measured and traffic conditions surveyed. Dames & Moore, consultants with HOK, conducted the very important environmental assessment, which was required by law before such a major construction project could be approved. Because the Metropolitan Washington Airports Authority had already studied this property as part of their own master planning exercise, there were some data available, but the requirements for an environmental assessment are numerous and very specific. Flora and fauna observations had to be taken during different seasons. Archeological findings could lead to other levels of examination. HOK had started this fieldwork before Congress instructed the Smithsonian to halt site-specific master planning. When the Dames & Moore team returned to the field in 1993, after President Clinton approved the project, they literally had to start most of their work over again. And findings had to be coordinated with the Corps of Engineers, environmental agencies from Virginia, the Environmental Protection Agency, and officials at Dulles. In February 1998, after many years of collecting data, producing reports, and sharing the information with the public through hearings, the FAA—the lead agency—declared that Dames & Moore had discovered nothing that would preclude the construction of NASM's new facility. The official verdict was a "finding of no significant impact."[23] This was one instance where insignificance was a good thing.

Who was coming to this new attraction, in what numbers, and from where? Yet another HOK consultant answered these questions in a very quantified fashion. The number of visitors was important because it would drive the sizing of several building and site components. How many parking spaces, restrooms, classrooms, dining tables, theater seats, and general circulation spaces should HOK work into the design. Harrison Price Company was hired to produce this important data. But NASM wasn't building a shopping mall or amusement park; the extension would not be a typical regional museum; the Dulles corridor was an area poised to grow with, and independent of, the airport. The Virginia Tourism Corporation had also crunched some numbers to come up with a visitor count for the Governor's office, and the initial work of the Air and Space Heritage Council had also included some educated speculations. But visitor projection is not an exact science, and the number of variables the Dulles study team had to consider was enormous. One important unknown was the type of and speed at which public transportation improvements would be made.

Harrison Price collected data from other attractions that could be considered comparable and queried transportation planners. Their report reflected by necessity a range of possible attendance levels, and the consultants downsized their numbers based on the scaled-back approach that Congress had directed NASM to take at Dulles. In their 1996 study, the experts predicted that with existing levels of public transportation (no rail or subway service between Washington and Dulles) the maximum attendance would be just over 2.5 million; with improved transportation, the number would climb to over 3 million. That translated into an estimated peak on-site crowd of 7,000 to 8,500.[24] The National Air and Space Museum already had experience with underestimating visitor numbers at its first facility, so project officials at NASM instructed HOK to design for 3 to 4 million visitors. Fortunately, at Dulles, there was more land onto which NASM could extend the parking lot and the buildings as needed if the visitor estimates were still too low. Financial planners were also interested in the projections as they figured revenue streams for the proposed theater, museum store, and food court. And transportation experts factored the numbers into their projections for traffic, pollution, and roadway upgrades.

In 1995, the Museum and its many supporters were treated to HOK's first concept drawings of the Dulles facility. Bill Hellmuth and his team of architects recommended a building that had three distinct zones. The easternmost section would be home to most of the basic visitor service features, as well as the large-screen theater, offices, and back-of-house functional spaces for building management. In the center of the design was a single large hangar with an arched roof that would house the aircraft collection. And on the west side, another hangar with a lower profile would be dedicated to the space artifacts, with an adjoining restoration hangar and storage space. A series of elevated walkways would allow visitors to see hanging artifacts and to watch restoration work in progress. With NASM staff, the architects had reviewed six building schemes, rejecting some, combining

This concept design was submitted in final form in
May 1996. Architect Bill Hellmuth described it:
"The building massing consists of three parts, the curved
transparent 'landside' building housing public amenities
and office space; a large hangar serving as the aviation
exhibit space; and a rectangular 'airside' building for space
hangar, restoration and storage. A strong cross axis
connects the pedestrian walkway from the parking areas,
through the main entrance hall, where a daylit circulation
spine draws visitors into the aviation exhibition hangar."

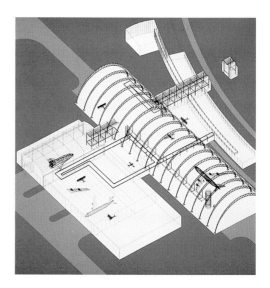

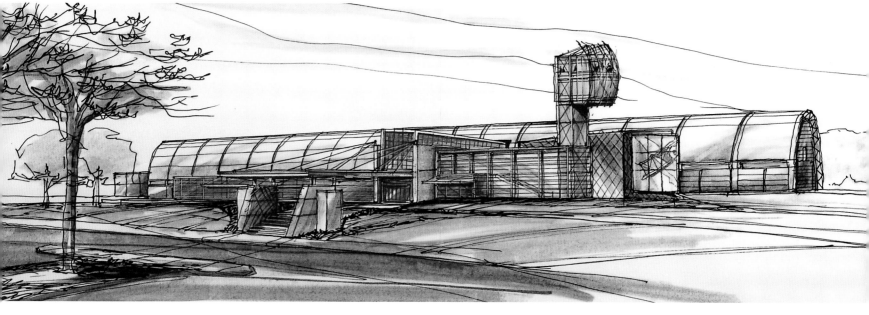

features of others, and narrowing the field to three. The collections crew approved of the "winning" design's dedicated spaces for the artifacts, segregated from the food service, entrance, and general loading dock. The architects saw the eastern wing of this design as an area that lent itself to more architectural expression and grander finishes than did the hangars. Clearly, the design accomplished the primary mission as defined during the master plan: "The intent is to provide museum quality care, storage, and protection for the collection while also providing access for visitors, educational groups and researchers."[25] HOK's design would accomplish that and more. The concept design—and all the design phases to follow—would also have to pass muster with the Metropolitan Washington Airports Authority. The Authority, not Fairfax County, would issue the Smithsonian a building permit and ensure that life and safety codes were met and that airport security was maintained.

As HOK and NASM were knee-deep in renderings and space requirement documents, the General Accounting Office was investigating the state of care the National Air and Space Museum was giving its aircraft. The study had been requested by Senator Kay Bailey Hutchinson. Authors of the 1996 report believed that NASM should reevaluate its collecting strategies, improve the

conditions of the Garber Facility, consider deaccessioning some objects, and expedite its plans for the Dulles Facility.[26] This advice came to NASM's new director, Admiral Don Engen, who was already running full steam ahead with the Dulles project. As Administrator of the FAA, he had approved the set-aside of land at Dulles for the Museum. He had been recruited for the Director's position, in part, because of his passion for flight and his solid connections with industry and with Congress. He was ready and able to expedite the fundraising required to build at Dulles. Congress had just passed another important authorization bill, giving the Smithsonian permission to construct the facility at Dulles when the design work was complete. But the law also specifically advised the Institution that no appropriated Federal funds would be used to pay any expense of construction. Even with Virginia's generous assistance with the site work, Engen believed that he needed to raise $100 million, a huge task for a museum with no organized capital campaign team in place. Congress had never before asked the Smithsonian to pay for such a huge project from private funds.

Engen's staff was completing the concept design and preparing for the next step—schematic design—when he offered his only design modification to the program. He was pleased with the hangar-like design; it looked like it

Above: Color renderings of the interior of the facility were required by the fundraising team to generate enthusiasm for the important content of the extension. Collections staff worked with the artist to ensure that all the details of the aircraft were correct.

Below: Aircraft restoration would be performed in full view of the public.

Bottom: The design team—and the fundraisers—never lost sight of the importance of education at the extension.

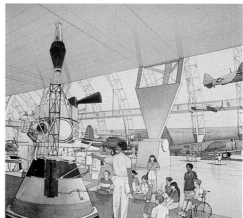

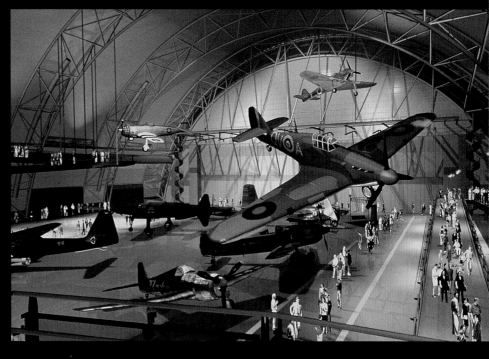

HOK contracted with Interface Multimedia to produce increasingly more realistic images of the exterior and interior of the facility. As the design work evolved, this talented company created computer visualizations from HOK's computer-aided design drawings. The artists at Interface added the right colors, shadows, reflectivity, and even visitors. Collections staffers Scott Wirz, Fran Tunstall, and Ed Mautner provided the details about the collections.

belonged at an airport, and it met the needs of the Museum. But any airport building of this stature needed a control tower. Bill Hellmuth was quick to supply one. When the first architectural model arrived at NASM, it had a removable tower for the north end of the entry wing. Project manager Ezell set up the model outside the Director's office when it arrived. The tower, along with small model aircraft and spacecraft, were in a box. Ezell positioned the artifacts in their appropriate places and showed Engen the model. Puzzled, he asked where the tower was. When Ezell explained that the tower was an option and not part of the core program for the

facility and was, therefore, still in the box, he made it perfectly clear to her that the tower would be the most important visual icon of the design and that it would be permanently glued onto the model. The tower was glued in place, and he was correct in his prediction. Engen also eliminated the word "extension" from the project's vocabulary. He hoped to eventually find someone whose donation would earn him naming rights, but until then the new facility would be known as the Dulles Center.

With every iteration of the design, HOK's cost estimate was further revised,

In July 1996 in the temporary hangar that housed the space shuttle *Enterprise* and a dozen large aircraft, Admiral Don Engen, with Senators Warner and Robb, unveiled the bill that would authorize construction of the Dulles Center. NASM Director Engen explained to Senator Warner how the building would accommodate some 200 aircraft and over 100 spacecraft.

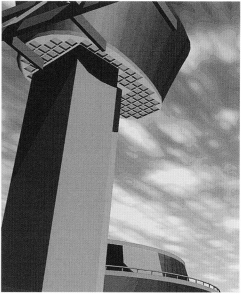

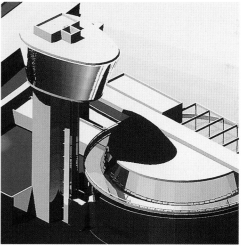

Architecturally, the observation tower was an eye-catching addition to the design.

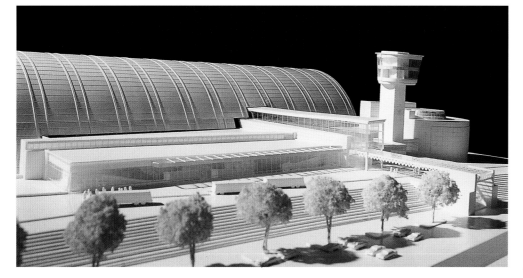

HOK and NASM further refined the design during 1998 and 1999, holding the line on any "program creep" but continuously moving interior spaces, carving room for mechanical-electrical-plumbing equipment, and adding more operational detail for the theater and other revenue-generating spaces. In the eastern wing, running from north to south on the entry level are the theater, observation tower, box office, welcome center desk, major donor recognition panels, lobby, museum store, food court, and office suite. On the ground level, near the theater and the entrance stairs were classrooms and offices for the education team; further south were offices and support spaces for building services, security, retail storage, and the loading dock. The large aviation hangar would accommodate aircraft on the floor and hanging at two levels. On the west, the space hangar was sized for the space shuttle. Next to it, the restoration hangar, with a series of specialty workshops and support spaces for the collections and exhibits crews, was visible to the public from level 2. The next unit of space housed the conservation lab, information technology, audio visual unit, and the archives on level 2 and collections receiving and processing on level 1. The final unit was dedicated to dense storage of collections not on display, including special areas for artwork and spacesuits. The facility's central utility plant was incorporated into the design of the western part of the building; it contained the chillers, boilers, and other equipment and automated systems that would ensure visitor comfort and a stable climate for the collection.

and the price kept going up. In late 1996, NASM formalized the relationship among the team members who had been interacting most closely with HOK. Ezell became the Dulles program manager; key staff from most of NASM's departments served with her as part of an interdisciplinary core team, some of whom would remain intimately involved with the project through move-in. Their first job was a painful one. Price had to be contained. What could be cut back, eliminated, or deferred? Melinda Humphry Becker, an architect with the Smithsonian, became the project's design manager, overseeing HOK's work now that the planning phase was complete.[27] She moved quickly to assist

the core team with identifying cuts and defending the strengths of the design. Al Bachmeier teamed with William "Jake" Jacobs, a NASM exhibits designer, to scrutinize every detail of the design, a task they would perform several times more before ground breaking. Sometimes the Museum cut space; sometimes it was special features that were dropped. But the team remained true to its highest priority; if it was related to the care of the collection, it remained in the program.

The schematic design report delivered in February 1997 and the design development reports of August 1997 provided more and more details,

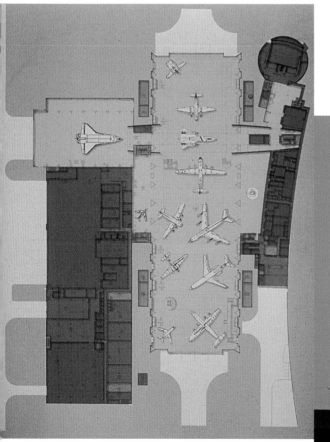

Floor plans and architectural elevations only hinted at the great potential of the building to protect the Air and Space Museum's valuable collections.

especially as regards the important mechanical-electrical-plumbing systems and the high-tech security systems specified by the Smithsonian. Those systems would add considerably to the cost of the building, but a stable, secure environment was critical to the Dulles Center's mission. By this time, the size of the facility had stabilized at about 63,810 square meters (709,000 sq ft). If the program had to be decreased in price further, some major program would have to go.

Admiral Don Engen did not live to see the Dulles Center built. He died in a glider accident in July 1999, as the design team's work on the 95 percent construction drawings was coming to an end. He had raised the visibility of the project among pilots, corporations, and government officials and pulled together a development crew that was charged with raising the money needed for construction. With Smithsonian Treasurer Sudeep Anand, he had devised several financial strategies that he hoped would get this project of national significance started. When the next NASM Director came to office, he would find the completed construction drawings on the shelf, with time racing by and the price of construction escalating.

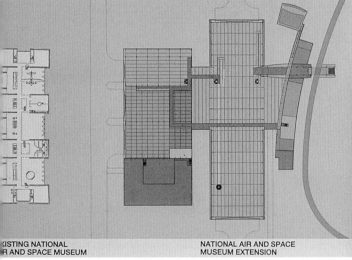

EXISTING NATIONAL
AIR AND SPACE MUSEUM   NATIONAL AIR AND SPACE
                                        MUSEUM EXTENSION

The Museum on the Mall in Washington, D.C., stretches three city blocks long, but it could fit comfortably inside the aviation hangar of the Dulles facility with room to spare.

Architect Bill Hellmuth and NASM Director Don Engen, on right, explain their vision for the design of the Dulles Center to senior Smithsonian managers, including Secretary I. Michael Heyman, center on left, in 1997.

CHAPTER THREE

Preparing the Site for the "Dulles Center"

CONCURRENT WITH DESIGNING THE BUILDING THAT WOULD HOUSE TREASURES FROM THE NATIONAL AIR AND SPACE MUSEUM AT WASHINGTON DULLES INTERNATIONAL AIRPORT, A GROUP OF CIVIL ENGINEERS AND ARCHITECTS WERE PLANNING THE BUILDING SITE, LANDSCAPING, AND ACCESS ROADS FOR THE DULLES CENTER. THE COMMONWEALTH OF VIRGINIA'S INVESTMENT IN THE MUSEUM'S VENTURE, FORMALIZED IN A MEMORANDUM OF INTENT IN APRIL 1990, CALLED FOR VIRGINIA TO CLEAR THE SITE, BRING IN UTILITIES, BUILD THE ROADS AND A TAXIWAY, PROVIDE THE LANDSCAPING, AND MITIGATE THE IMPACT OF ANY WETLANDS DISTURBANCE THAT RESULTED FROM THIS WORK. SINCE ACCESSIBILITY FOR THE PUBLIC AS WELL AS FOR ARRIVING AIRCRAFT WAS CRITICAL TO THE SUCCESS OF THE FACILITY, HELLMUTH, OBATA + KASSABAUM'S (HOK) TEAM STUDIED THE OPTIONS CAREFULLY WITH THE VIRGINIA DEPARTMENT OF TRANSPORTATION (VDOT). MANAGERS, FINANCIAL EXPERTS, AND ENGINEERS FROM VDOT WERE CHARGED WITH TRANSLATING VIRGINIA'S GENEROSITY INTO A COMPLETED PROJECT AT DULLES.

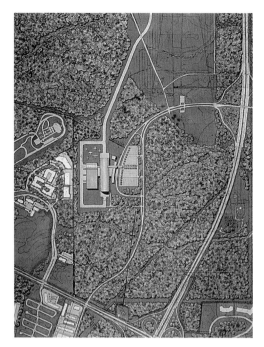

HOK's first site plan called for the visitor entrance off Route 28, from the east; the taxiway, or "haul road," to Runway 1R-19L ran directly north; an apron wrapped around the hangars on three sides; and a secondary entrance ran due south to Route 50.   ·

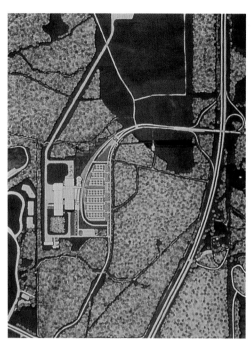

With the help of the Corps of Engineers, HOK positioned the building and roads so that wetland impacts would be kept to a minimum. And the Airports Authority eliminated an area for aircraft viewing along the entrance road in the interest of security, a decision that was validated in 2001 with the need for enhanced security at all U.S. airports.

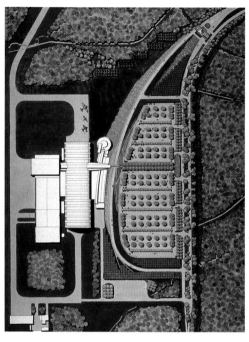

Suzette Voline Goldstein of HOK led the team that designed the landscape. The designers minimized disruption of the site and developed a naturally sustainable landscape for the entrance. From the interchange to the parking toll plaza, the area would be planted in grasses and wild flowers. Closer to the building, the design became more formal.

Site Design

T HE EARLIEST feasibility studies had suggested that building construction should start on the northern half of the large site identified for the Museum by the Metropolitan Washington Airports Authority (MWAA), which, when surveyed, was logged in at 71.5 hectares (176.5 acres). A risk analysis, based on historical data, had plotted where aircraft accidents were most likely to occur at airports like Dulles, and the Museum's new home was deemed safe.[1] On the north end, the first buildings would be closer to Runway 1R-19L, making it easier and more economical to get large aircraft and the space shuttle *Enterprise* to their new home. HOK's civil engineering partner, Patton Harris Rust & Associates, concurred with this strategy. Two roads into the project would be needed, one from the south off Route 50 for construction access and later for Museum operations and the primary roadway from Route 28, which would also necessitate the construction of a long-planned interchange. A limited taxiway would run north to the runway, wide enough for the largest commercial and military aircraft the Museum intended to display.

From environmental assessment fieldwork and surveys of the property, the architects knew the precise lay of the land. While no endangered or protected species had been discovered, the team recognized the importance of the open habitat, across which the

primary road would be built, and it was imperative that the minimum number of wetlands be disturbed during construction.[2] And it was a goal, although not required by law, to avoid sites that had given up archeological artifacts. Except along Cain's Branch stream, the soil was found to be uniformly red, silty clay. Law Engineering's geotechnical investigation had discovered siltstone, mudstone, sandstone, and shale beneath the surface layer. Depth to bedrock ranged from the

surface down to about 6 meters (20 ft) and promised to challenge any future drilling crews. Considering all these factors, HOK's site planners identified two possible areas for the building on the northern half of the property, and they looked at two alternatives for the taxiway, which the Federal Aviation Administration now labeled a "haul road" for aircraft.[3]

The U.S. Army Corps of Engineers regulates most stream channels in the

United States, and with this responsibility comes the task of approving construction plans that affect wetlands. Wetlands are identified by three parameters: certain plants, like swamp rose, ferns, and common green briar, grow there; wetlands do not drain well; and water is often present at or above ground surface. There are two categories: emergent and forested. The Smithsonian identified about 10 hectares (25 acres) of wetlands scattered throughout the parcel of land set aside

Wetlands Mitigation

To mitigate damage to the region's environmental balance caused by disturbances to wetlands during construction, the U.S. Army Corps of Engineers requires that damaged wetlands be replaced or restored in the same watershed. The Corps uses a complex formula to determine how many new hectares (acres) of wetlands must be created, which factors in the types of wetlands disturbed and their extent. In the case of the Smithsonian's project at Dulles, the Corps told the Institution that it was required to create 6 new hectares (15 acres) of wetlands in return for disturbing 3 hectares (7 acres). There were no opportunities for creating wetlands at Dulles Airport. The Airports Authority itself would need to mitigate wetland disturbances that resulted from constructing new runways and terminals and would not allow the Smithsonian to use up any such opportunities for mitigation on site. Smithsonian staff sought other public lands in the Dulles area for wetlands work and investigated the possibility of purchasing wetlands credits.

One morning en route to the airport, the Smithsonian team was discussing the problem so intensely that they missed their exit on Route 66 for Dulles. When they noticed their lapse, the first exit they could take to turn around was marked "Manassas National Battlefield Park." That afternoon program manager Lin Ezell called National Park Service Superintendent Robert Sutton to discuss the possibility of creating or restoring wetlands at the Manassas battlefield. The Park had long wanted to restore an area called Stuart's Hill to its 1860s configuration. This tract had been disturbed by a developer before it was annexed by the Park, but a University of Georgia School of Design study provided a good roadmap for how to restore it. Included in the plan was the recreation of wetlands. With the Corps' agreement, the Smithsonian restored the easternmost 18 hectares (45 acres) of Stuart's Hill. Land was contoured, drainage elevations sculpted, and specific vegetation planted. Dames & Moore and URS Corp. designed the project, as part of the HOK team. The work was performed in 2003 by Environmental Quality Resources, with funding provided by Virginia. For five years, the Park Service and the Smithsonian will closely monitor the land to ensure that it is performing according to the design requirements for viable wetlands, while the public enjoys access to this important Civil War property.

for Air and Space. With the help of Corps of Engineers district officer Ron Stouffer, HOK skillfully manipulated the design of roads, utility trenches, taxiway, and building site to impact only about 3 hectares (7 acres). Securing a wetlands permit from the Corps is a major hurdle for any construction project. The Smithsonian had outstanding cooperation from the Corps' Northern Virginia District Office and from the Virginia Department of Environmental Quality, which made its own independent assessments and also granted approval to construct.

Designs for the utilities, roadways, new intersection, and taxiway, as well as the plan of attack for clearing the site, had to pass inspection by Smithsonian staff, Airports Authority engineers and security personnel, Fairfax County Water Authority, and the Virginia Department of Transportation, which would be letting contracts for the work and overseeing those construction projects alongside the Smithsonian's other contractors. VDOT was concerned, of course, about good engineering, but the agency was also charged with keeping the project within the scope of the Commonwealth's intent to help—and the advertised budget.[4] For example, when the Smithsonian suggested it needed landscaping around the building that exceeded the norm for highway projects, an allowance was established for Virginia's portion of the landscaping; beyond that allowance, the Museum would need to add to the pot, which it did. To coordinate all the many layers of reviews and nuances of site work and to track the complicated finances, Smithsonian architect David Hay was enlisted to assist design manager Melinda Humphry Becker and project manager Sheryl Kolasinski within the Smithsonian's Office of Physical Plant.

VDOT divided the site work into several

distinct packages. Obviously, the first thing needed was to clear the site, and crews would carve a construction access road in from the south. The labor-intensive job of installing utilities, with its extensive system of underground trenches, would stretch over many months. The second site contractor would complete the utilities work and pave the roads, taxiway, and parking lot. The intersection would be constructed by a third team. And the final package, wetlands mitigation, would be accomplished off-site at nearby Manassas National Battlefield Park. Virginia was ready with the design and the funding to clear the airport site by late 1998. The Smithsonian, however, was not yet ready to build.

Officials from the Smithsonian and the Metropolitan Washington Airports Authority gathered on November 12, 1998, at the National Air and Space Museum to witness the signing of a long-term lease for the property on which the Dulles Center would be built. Admiral Don Engen, NASM Director, and Jim Wilding, President and CEO of MWAA, agreed to terms that, with extensions, would guarantee the Museum a second home midway through the next century. Engineers, planners, project managers, financial staff, and lawyers from both organizations attended.

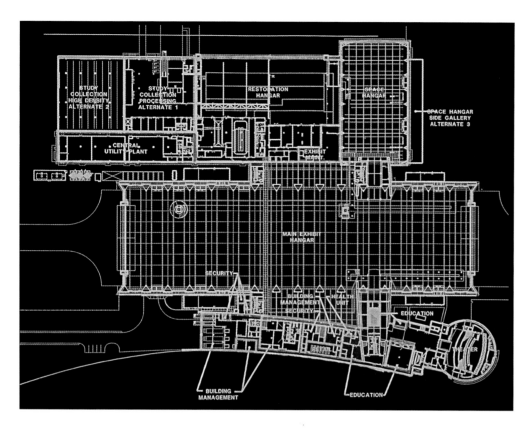

HOK and NASM pared back the "base building" to 63,900 square meters (710,000 sq ft) to make construction more affordable. On this drawing, options (or "alternates") in addition to the "base building" are marked as study collection and processing (this also included a conservation lab and archives on level 2); collection high-density (for artifacts in the study collection), and space hangar gallery (an extension of the larger space hangar).

Phasing the project, however, would not change the outward appearance of the facility from the perspective of visitors heading up the front driveway.

Building Design Revisited

Senior managers at the Smithsonian carefully guarded the Institution's financial integrity. Stock market volatility during the late 1990s had prompted some potential contributors to rethink their philanthropic strategies, and Smithsonian treasurer Sudeep Anand constantly evaluated the Institution's fiscal worth and analyzed what risks it could take with financing new projects, in partnership with Elizabeth Scheffler, Associate Director for Operations at NASM. In addition to the Air and Space Museum's project at Dulles, the Smithsonian was also designing the National Museum of the American Indian, and other costly building restoration projects were under review. The Smithsonian did not want Virginia to proceed with building a road to a construction site that would remain untouched for some time due to lack of funding. NASM and other Smithsonian officials carefully calculated projected revenues, turned up the pressure on its capital campaign, and calculated short- and long-term debt scenarios. In 1999, the project's budget was listed at $160 million: $130 million for the building and $30 million for the site work provided by Virginia. What could be done to decrease costs?

HOK had substantially completed its 100 percent construction documents in March 1999. During its review of those many volumes of specifications and drawings and the latest revision of the cost estimate, the Smithsonian recommended a drastic solution: study a phased approach to building the Dulles Center. They should cut up the building, which was now sized at 68,400 square metres (760,000 sq ft). HOK's design, with its three distinct zones, lent itself to subdividing. NASM's core team had already spent many months agonizing over how to repackage the design and scale back their needs for opening and operating the facility, an exercise that took its toll on morale and encouraged the nay-sayers who predicted that the long-held dream would not become reality. The Smithsonian was being assisted in this painful work by Parsons Brinckerhoff Construction Services. Parsons had already signed on to provide construction management services in the field at Dulles. For now, however, Parsons was helping with constructability reviews, and the support team would assist in the evaluation of technical proposals from prospective builders of the new facility when the time came.

The newly defined "base building" would include the eastern wing with its public spaces, theater, and tower, the aviation hangar, the entire central utility plant, the restoration hangar, and most of the space hangar. Other pieces of the building were labeled as options, which could be built as additional funding became available. Option number one included the west-side collections processing unit, conservation laboratory, and archives. The second option contained the study collection storage unit, while several other options described minor building features or additions that could be deferred or dropped. It was also discovered that the

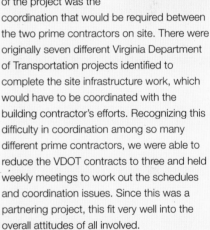

From the Field

Paul Dickens, Project Manager, Parsons Brinckerhoff Construction Services

One of the very first things Parsons Brinckerhoff recognized during constructability reviews prior to the start of the project was the coordination that would be required between the two prime contractors on site. There were originally seven different Virginia Department of Transportation projects identified to complete the site infrastructure work, which would have to be coordinated with the building contractor's efforts. Recognizing this difficulty in coordination among so many different prime contractors, we were able to reduce the VDOT contracts to three and held weekly meetings to work out the schedules and coordination issues. Since this was a partnering project, this fit very well into the overall attitudes of all involved.

This was truly a unique project. It was one of those "once in a lifetime" efforts, and all parties assembled a great "project team" that worked well together. All parties—from the owner, the user, the contractors and subs, down to the individual workers—had a "can do" mentality to getting the work done.

central utility plant had even more capacity than would be required for the entire complex, so the Smithsonian added an option that would actually increase the cost of the project: adding to the length—and volume—of the aviation hangar. HOK calculated the new base building to be 63,900 square meters (710,000 sq ft). Everyone wondered what the new market price would actually be for this downsized Dulles Center.

During the late summer of 1999, the Museum found a new friend, and the timing was ideal. Steven F. Udvar-Hazy, chairman, chief executive officer, and founder of International Lease Finance Corp. of Los Angeles, discussed his family's wishes to support the National Air and Space Museum over a lunch with Acting Director Don Lopez after visiting the Paul Garber Facility. In October, he announced a pledge of $60 million for

NASM Director Jack Dailey wanted the new museum to open in December 2003, in time to mark 100 years of manned powered flight. The Wright brothers demonstrated that man could fly at Kitty Hawk, North Carolina, on December 17, 1903. An entire century of progress would be on display at Dulles.

the Dulles Center, the largest single gift to date for a Smithsonian project. Udvar-Hazy wrote to Lopez: "All my life, I have been committed to aviation and the industry's advancements and development, and it is an honor for my family and company to solidify the museum's mission of restoring, preserving and displaying our aviation heritage."[5] The Museum had already raised $28 million, working toward the $130 million goal. This substantial gift from the Udvar-Hazy family energized the campaign team and the Museum's National Board and inspired NASM's next director.

When General John R. "Jack" Dailey became NASM's director in early 2000, the problem of raising the remaining funds for the Dulles Center was placed squarely on his desk. The team in the field wanted to clear the site that spring to put the project on track for completion to mark a date important to the aviation community. On December 17, 2003, the world would commemorate the hundredth anniversary of the first manned powered flight by the Wright brothers at Kitty Hawk, North Carolina. General Dailey intended for that celebration to be marked in style at the new facility at Dulles. With the promise of the Udvar-Hazy gift and the scaled-back approach to building, the Smithsonian advised Virginia that the state could proceed with bidding the first package of site work at Dulles for the National Air and Space Museum's Steven F. Udvar-Hazy Center. And the Office of Contracting got into high gear with assembling the bid package for the construction of the building to meet an anticipated January 2001 start date.

Site Construction—Act 1

The Virginia Department of Transportation had a loyal following of contractors in northern Virginia who could be counted on to bid on most of the agency's traditional highway jobs. Interest in the first site package for the Air and Space Museum project also ran high. Cherry Hill Construction Company was the winning bidder. Even as the heavy construction team managers took their seats at the July 12 pre-construction meeting, the Museum had a special request. Formal groundbreaking would take place in October near the building pad, and all those dignitaries would need a road in place to get there.

The $7.49 million-package of work was scheduled to run for less than 9 months. Because of the magnitude of the Dulles project, the Smithsonian assigned two construction managers to the job. That summer, Vince Cogliano and George Golden took up residency in construction trailers, along with their colleagues from VDOT, to oversee the site work. Rick Miller led the VDOT team.

In mid-May 2000, the Smithsonian released a request for proposals for the building contract. The Institution was seeking the best technical proposal and price from a general contractor who could turn HOK's construction drawings and NASM's dreams into steel and concrete. The interested bidders had 90 days to prepare their bids, and they got their first look at the construction site at Dulles in mid-June. Initial bids were due in August, with best and final prices by September.

While the project team in Washington worked on answers to the bidders' questions and listened to technical presentations that summer, the civil engineers continued to work on the finishing touches of the next two site design packages.

It was already obvious to the Smithsonian and Parsons that coordinating the efforts of two families of contractors—VDOT's site teams and the Smithsonian's general contractor—would be a challenge, and they wanted the design documents to be complete in every detail. It could be difficult to always know where one contractor's work ended and another's began.

Paul Dickens, Parsons' project manager for Dulles, predicted that the large site would seem much smaller once some 600 workers started swarming over it. HOK would be there, too, with a small number of architects to provide construction administration services, helping the general contractor and the Smithsonian with the details and scrambling to get fast answers to questions from the field. Smithsonian construction managers Cogliano and Golden, design managers Humphry Becker and Hay, and NASM project coordinator Ezell divided their time between the conference rooms of the Victor Building in Washington, D.C., where the Smithsonian's engineers, project managers, and architects were housed, and construction trailers at Dulles in anticipation of a speedy contract award.[6]

Heavy construction operators under contract to the Virginia Department of Transportation got into high gear to clear the site in time for an official groundbreaking ceremony scheduled for the fall of 2000.

Old farm fields had long been replaced by stands of pine trees along the southern boundary of Dulles Airport, which were harvested by Cherry Hill Construction Co. as part of their site work during the summer of 2000. This lone fence post, discovered on the west side of the site, was the only reminder of the crops and livestock that once thrived at the site of the Museum's project.

By late summer, most of the site needed for immediate construction had been cleared and grubbed of trees, vegetation, roots, and debris.

Cherry Hill literally had to blast their way into the site to build the construction access road off Route 50 to the south. Each blast had to be coordinated with the airport operations staff.

Protecting Cain's Branch stream from pollution and the surrounding properties from construction run-off was required by the Virginia Department of Environmental Quality. The perennial stream and its banks were already part of an environmental quality corridor that could not be built on, but the southern road and a western jeep path both had to cross the water. They were protected during construction by temporary silt fences, which were patrolled regularly. Huge double and triple box culverts were craned into place to serve as the permanent guards. Before a crane could raise its boom, airport officials had to be advised so that aircraft coming in on approach to Runway 1R-19L would know of the activity.

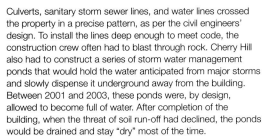

Culverts, sanitary storm sewer lines, and water lines crossed the property in a precise pattern, as per the civil engineers' design. To install the lines deep enough to meet code, the construction crew often had to blast through rock. Cherry Hill also had to construct a series of storm water management ponds that would hold the water anticipated from major storms and slowly dispense it underground away from the building. Between 2001 and 2003, these ponds were, by design, allowed to become full of water. After completion of the building, when the threat of soil run-off had declined, the ponds would be drained and stay "dry" most of the time.

Cherry Hill moved thousands of cubic meters of dirt and rock in 2000–2001 to sculpt the land so that its elevations were precise to ensure proper drainage and to meet the architects' plans for how the building was to be positioned. In many areas, soil had to be removed to lower the elevations; some of that material was moved to other areas on site that needed fill. The ideal site achieves balance between what is "cut" and what is "filled." If it does not, the project pays to bring in more soil or pays to haul off what is excess to the job. Project engineers were hopeful that the growing mountains of removed dirt and rock would be required for the construction of the interchange or for other projects at the airport.

Cherry Hill's crews performed most of their utility work underground, although much-needed temporary power came into the site on poles during the summer of 2001.

Banks of ductwork snaked their way across the site, bringing in electrical and communications service for the building. Gas lines also had to be placed within the utility easements and carefully marked.

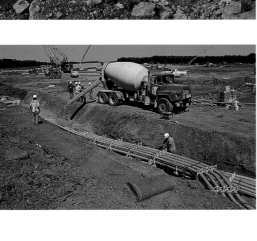

Contractors delivered a graveled roadway through the pine forest
for the groundbreaking ceremony in October 2000.

Site crews also cut access paths through the trees north to
the runway and east to Route 28 where a new interchange
would be built.

Winter weather in 2000–2001 called a halt to the power parade of heavy equipment that was preparing the building pad on which the Udvar-Hazy Center would be constructed.

There was enough fair weather for crews to grade, gravel, level, and compact the pad so that it was ready for the general contractor in mid-2001. And always workers were treated to the regular pattern of arriving and departing aircraft from Dulles' nearby runways.

Rocky soil had to be supplemented with topsoil, screened on site and planted with grass seed, to stabilize areas near the building pad and roads, preventing erosion and run-off. Cherry Hill's last task was to install permanent fencing around the 71.5-hectare (176.5-acre) site to meet airport security requirements and to protect the valuable artifacts that would soon call Dulles home.

Above: The northern half of the Museum's site at Washington Dulles International Airport was largely cleared by the fall of 2000.

Below: Formal groundbreaking ceremonies were held on October 25, 2000.

The Culture of Design

The first things you notice about HOK's offices in Georgetown in Washington, D.C., are the light streaming in from huge windows overlooking the C&O Canal, hardwood floors, and exposed brick from earlier centuries left by the building's restorers. Architects have papered every possible wall with a chaotic and colorful array of photographs, posters, sketches of works in progress, and material samples. On two large floors, dozens of architects, engineers, planners, artists, and support personnel bustle. The offices always hum with energy. No one sits still for long, and young staff scoot on their chairs throughout the warren of open cubicles for impromptu consultations. Stacks of bound drawings, discarded and current models, bricks, panes of glass, and swatches of material are on tables, in corners, and underfoot. Desks are anchored with the latest computers and piled high with paper, color markers, rules, and pens. And every architect has close at hand a roll of tracing paper so that the latest idea for a change can be sketched over the face of a drawing, discarded, and sketched again. It is a dynamic place, strange and almost bohemian at first for visitors from the Air and Space Museum. It would become their second home.

If you plotted the corporate personality profiles of HOK and NASM, you would find HOK draped over one corner of the grid and NASM precisely lined up in regimental form in the opposite corner. In part because the Museum had lived with the problems associated with inadequate space for its collections for so long and in part because the staff was very technically astute, the Museum knew exactly what it wanted from the architects when the two parties first met. And Museum staff weren't shy about telling them. While the breadth of the program waxed and waned over time with changing directors and budgets, the core of the need always centered on the requirements of the collection, and it was the collections-focused members of the NASM team who had the most intense and longest-lasting relationship with HOK. And they were very technically inclined.

From the beginning, the NASM team thought and spoke in terms of how much space was needed and for what, how thick the concrete floors of the hangars should be, what the roof should be made of, how artifacts should be hung and from where, how wide the doors should be, where electrical outlets were needed, and just how the mechanical systems should work. They could already see the new facility in their heads, and they knew how it should operate and how desperately it was needed. The architects spoke in very different terms. At meetings, they talked about scoping, adjacencies, the strong axis of the building, texture, nose-to-nose experiences with the artifacts, how the building "spoke" to them, and how the building "wanted to do" this or that. While the two cultures didn't clash, they certainly bumped into one another from time to time as they worked together closely over so many years.

The architects listened keenly to the Museum's needs and gave the customer the functionality they asked for, and they really had no choice in the

matter. But they also worked beauty and grace into the building's design. As cost estimates crept up, the Museum gave extra scrutiny to anything it considered extraneous or grand, and the architects, in turn, defended their design, materials, and finishes. Many compromises were struck by the Smithsonian's skillful design managers, who understood what the architects were trying to achieve artistically but appreciated the basic needs of the Museum. While every final material, color, and nuance of each space was documented, reviewed, and approved by the Smithsonian in the construction drawings, some of the team members who had been most closely involved were often surprised in the field as the building grew from footers and steel into finished spaces. HOK clearly had a vision for the Udvar-Hazy Center that combined the unique requirements of the Museum with a subtle grandeur that fits the ambience of the airport environment perfectly. And while the building never actually spoke to the Museum, it did sing when strong afternoon winds blew through steel structure not yet enclosed.

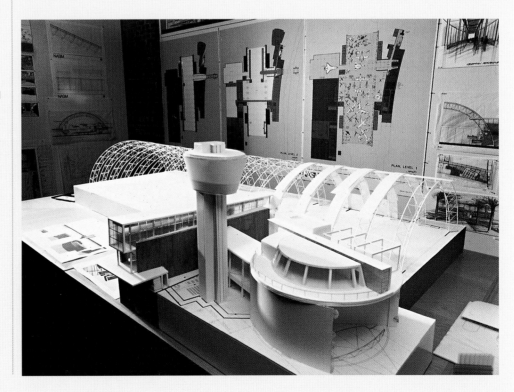

CHAPTER FOUR

Building the Steven F. Udvar-Hazy Center

IN RESPONSE TO THE SPRING 2000 REQUEST FOR PROPOSALS FROM GENERAL CONTRACTORS INTERESTED IN BUILDING THE UDVAR-HAZY CENTER, SEVEN CONTRACTORS INDICATED THEIR INTEREST IN BIDDING. THE SMITHSONIAN'S OFFICE OF CONTRACTING (OCON) HAD SENT INFORMATION ON THIS HIGH-PROFILE PROJECT TO MORE THAN 40 GENERAL CONTRACTORS AROUND THE COUNTRY WITH ENOUGH ALLEGED EXPERIENCE TO BRING BUILDINGS COSTING MORE THAN $100 MILLION IN ON TIME, ON BUDGET, WITH HIGH QUALITY. OF THE SEVEN, THREE COMPANIES, ALL BASED IN THE WASHINGTON, D.C., REGION, SUBMITTED BID PACKAGES.[1] IT WAS A BOOM TIME FOR CONSTRUCTION IN THE AREA, ESPECIALLY IN THE DULLES CORRIDOR. DULLES AIRPORT, ALONE, HAD $800 MILLION WORTH OF NEW CONSTRUCTION "ON THE STREET" WAITING FOR BIDS. SOME INTERESTED CONTRACTORS, THEIR RESOURCES ALREADY STRETCHED TO CAPACITY, WERE FORCED TO DROP OUT OF THE COMPETITION BEFORE IT BEGAN.

Completing the Team

CONTRACTORS had been tasked with addressing three broad topics in their technical proposals: plan of accomplishment and schedule; key personnel and their subcontractor team; and the firm's experience and past performance. Cost proposals were to be submitted separately, and two independent Smithsonian teams would evaluate the technical and financial information. John Cobert, director of the Smithsonian's contracting office, told the interested contractors that the Institution had estimated the job at $105–125 million, and price was literally half the battle. The technical proposal and the cost proposal were each worth 50 points during evaluation. For the technical proposal, plan and schedule were worth 20 points, personnel 10, and experience 20. And there was a schedule spelled out in the documents. Working from west to east, the National Air and Space Museum (NASM) wanted to have the restoration hangar completed by July 1, 2002, the aviation hangar by early 2003, and the east wing by early December, in time for the mid-December opening.[2]

Even before the first visit to the site, the contractors were told of some changes, in the form of addendums, to the scope

Space hangar construction lagged behind the rest of the project, but funding from the James S. McDonnell Foundation ensured its completion, too, for the opening in December 2003.

of the project. They were asked to submit prices for upgraded mechanical systems in the event that the Museum extended the length of the aviation hangar some day. John Safer, a local sculptor and friend of the Museum, had donated a major sculpture for the entrance; what would it cost to build a base and fountain for it? And there was the possibility that solar panels would be incorporated into the building if a proposed donation came through; what would that do to price and schedule?[3] With offers due in August and award in October, everyone was scrambling.

The technical evaluation team that would study the proposals was small and included representatives from the Smithsonian's design and construction team and NASM, with staff from Hellmuth, Obata + Kassabaum (HOK) and Parsons Brinckerhoff assisting. It was the same team that had been working together closely for several years. Proposals were delivered by the boxful in late August. Strict confidentiality was imposed, and the many binders full of proposal details were kept under lock and key at the Office of Physical Plant in the Victor Building in downtown Washington. Several rooms were turned over for the team, which set to work.

Evaluation guidelines suggested that the construction schedule should include at least 250 separate activities representing all the critical elements of work, including foundations and structure, building and fit-out, phased milestones, substantial completion dates, and final completion. Critical paths toward completion needed to be clearly marked. And it was estimated that the contractor should take no more than 870 days to build the Center. Other points of interest that the team looked for were the contractors' plans to interact with Virginia's site contractors and with the Museum once artifact move-in commenced—before the building was even finished! Working in close quarters together would require understanding and trust.

Nineteen areas of work had to be addressed in the contractors' implementation plans. They were instructed to describe "in detail the particular procedures, site strategy, and work methodology planned for this project that will deliver a superior quality product...."[4] The list was an outline of the pieces and parts of the building:

Sitework

Hardscape

Landscape

Concrete

Structural steel and framing

Hangar doors

Roofing

Air/vapor barrier and insulation

Structural sealant glazing

Finishes

Plumbing and heating/cooling

Electrical

Fire protection

Elevators

Security systems

Furnishings

Telecommunications

A/V and theater

Signage

In mid-September, the six-person technical evaluation panel, along with colleagues who had also read every document and submitted informal

Contractors bidding on the job addressed 19 specialties that would be required to construct the new museum at Dulles.

Opposite: Structural steel for the aviation hangar was one of the long lead-time items that the contractors had to plan for as they prepared—and held—their bids.

summary evaluations, tallied the vote. Two of the three scored very closely; the remaining contractor placed third. Each had a distinct management style; each had a distinct plan of attack. And all were invited to give a presentation to the technical team and answer questions in late September.

The three potential contractors had all worked hard to prepare for the technical presentations. They brought models, more schedules and handouts, and computer-projected slides. Each team was composed of a hierarchy of staff, and, although the titles varied, the roles were the same: high-ranking senior manager, project superintendent, cost estimator, project manager, and general foreman—all dressed according to their station. Interviews one and two were similar in structure. The presentations had been rehearsed and polished; each player had a definite role and stuck to the script. Questions were asked and answered successfully. The final presenters came into the session with fewer props, less structure, and less polish. It seemed that all members of the third team knew one another's areas of expertise and that they had been living this project together intensely. In their enthusiasm, they interrupted one another, explored ideas, and answered the Smithsonian's questions about related projects they had built. After one more round of written questions and answers between OCon and the proposers, the technical evaluation team unanimously concurred in mid-October. They recommended the company they believed to be the best qualified to build at Dulles, but could the Smithsonian afford it?

No. The Smithsonian could not allow the project to assume long-term debt for construction. While the $60 million-gift of the previous year and continued fundraising had given Director Jack Dailey confidence in the Museum's ability to build the entire project, he did not have all the cash and pledges in hand to start building. Smithsonian Secretary Lawrence M. Small told him to study the options. NASM could wait until more money had been raised and start the bidding process over again, but the first 100 years of powered flight might not be celebrated at the new facility with such a delay. NASM could lower its standards and save money on the expensive mechanical systems and other features that helped protect the collection, but that was unacceptable. The team could conduct another value engineering exercise in an attempt to shave costs, but they had dedicated most of 1998 to that aim and didn't believe they could find much more to cut. Or NASM could redefine the base building and defer more building blocks to subsequent phases of construction. As the Smithsonian studied its options, the contractors with bids on the table held fast but grew nervous. The teams they had dedicated to the project were marching in place; they had forged partnerships with subcontractors; they had time-sensitive quotes on materials with long lead times. Jack Dailey visited all three contractors in mid-November and asked them to extend their bids for an additional 120 days, until late March 2001.[5] They all agreed.

By late in the year, the Smithsonian agreed that the only approach that would guarantee opening by December 2003 was to pare the project back

further, divide it into more parts that could be priced separately. This was a difficult decision for the Museum. Structurally, it made sense to defer the entire western "third" of the design: space hangar, restoration hangar, collections processing-archives-conservation lab, and collections storage. All four components were critical to managing the collections, but none could be afforded for opening day. Not having a restoration hangar to work from would make moving the artifacts in especially challenging. It was difficult to keep staff morale high at NASM, knowing that a major part of the project would likely be deferred.

HOK suffered the most pressure. Eight volumes of drawings had to be repackaged to reflect these new options. And in a gutsy move, Dailey also instructed HOK to include the option for four additional "bays" for the aviation hangar—a price increase. His confidence level remained high. He stated repeatedly that this country would not let them down, that "America's Hangar" would be built, all of it.

It was early March before the architects had made all the required changes to the construction documents that reflected a smaller base building and 10 alternates. As newly defined, the Center would include most of the public areas and most of the revenue-generating features, which were important to the financial planners. Earned revenue would help pay down short-term debt against pledges of donations. New offers were submitted by all three general contractors; the technical panel's findings were the same, delivered in mid-March. Again, it was a matter of price. How much short-term

debt was the Smithsonian comfortable with holding? How aggressively could the capital campaign for Udvar-Hazy funding be waged?

Sheila Burke, Under Secretary for American Museums and National Programs, agreed with Jack Dailey that it was not practical to wait until all the money had been raised before starting construction. In fact, a project under way should inspire other leadership gifts. In late March, she told the members of the executive committee of the Board of Regents that a phased approach to building the Udvar-Hazy Center "offers unique opportunities to entice potential donors and gives us additional time for fund raising to pay for other aspects of the project. This approach also limits the Institutional exposure to unreasonable financial risk." She recommended that the project be approved. The cost estimates for the first phase—building construction, Virginia's site work, raising funds, financing, and move-in/start-up—had come in at $200.23 million. Current support was calculated at $150.21 million, with $50 million to be funded through future earnings. It was a limited risk. The Regents agreed with Burke on March 28. The next day, the Smithsonian awarded the contract for the first phase of construction to Hensel Phelps Construction Company for $125,578,000.[6] The price included the extra mechanical system work and additional site features that were beyond the scope of Virginia's assistance. It would require major hustle by all parties to complete the aviation hangar by early 2003 so the Museum could start moving in. Opening day remained fixed: in time to celebrate the Wright brothers' accomplishments.

Hensel Phelps Builds a Strong Foundation

In late spring 2001, Hensel Phelps started foundation work for the large-format theater. The theater would anchor the east wing on the north end. HPCC named Bruce Rosenthal area superintendent for the east wing of the building, which would also include the observation tower, classrooms, museum store, and food court.

Hensel Phelps, as general contractor, had sole contractual responsibility for the delivery of the finished building on schedule and to specification. But the Colorado-based company would not "self-perform" all the work. They would bring to the field scores of their own crafts people, as well as subcontractors and vendors for whom Hensel Phelps would be responsible (see Appendix 1 for a list of contractors who contributed to the project and Appendix 2 for a summary design and construction schedule). In advance of submitting their bid to the Smithsonian, the general contractor had negotiated many deals of its own with specialists in every area, from the steel fabricator who would erect the giant arches of the aviation hangar to the vendor who would supply hazardous material storage lockers. They all became part of the Hensel Phelps team.

Hensel Phelps Construction Company (HPCC) is an employee-owned company, established in 1937 and based in Greeley, Colorado. Large one-of-a-kind structures are their specialty. Of interest to the technical evaluation team had been their work building hangars for United, American, and Continental Airlines and terminals at several airports, including Dulles. By constructing aquariums, sports arenas, and convention centers, HPCC had gained experience with owners who served large numbers of visitors with high expectations. The Air

Safety—in the air erecting giant steel arches or on the ground installing utilities—was all-important to the construction team.

and Space Museum job was bid by the mid-Atlantic regional office, opened in 1996 in Chantilly, Virginia, less than a mile from Dulles Airport. Executive Vice President Bob Daniels, who led the Chantilly office, was a pilot who appreciated the history of aviation. He had been watching the Smithsonian project for several years, waiting for a chance to bid on it. His father had flown on B-17s in the China-Burma-India theater in World War II, and Daniels very much wanted this new museum to be a testament to the achievements of that generation.

To house the many staff who would be needed on site, industrial-sized tow trucks started bringing in office trailers, which were lined up in rows well south of the building pad. A small trailer village grew up there, next to one of the storm water management ponds and backed up to the woods along Cain's Branch stream. The view to the north toward the building changed almost every day, and with it came a non-stop parade of heavy equipment, delivery trucks, and construction crews, often enveloped in a cloud of red dust or stuck in red mud or snow. Out the backs of the trailers, it was almost serene. You could glimpse a fox trotting across the power easement, deer—at least two albinos were spotted over the course of the project—or blue heron visiting the pond when it held water. Parsons Brinckerhoff, as part of their construction management duties, arranged for the Smithsonian's two trailers. The first one was set up next to the general contractors' three trailers, all connected together by wooden decks. Major subcontractors brought in their own trailers to serve as home base for

their crews and to store material and equipment. At the height of the project, more than 30 large trailers lined the lower apron road or lay scattered elsewhere on the site.

One of the first mobile offices to be up and running belonged to Hensel Phelps' safety officer. Safety was one of the general contractor's core values. Absolutely everyone who worked—or walked—on the project site was required to take a safety class or be escorted by someone who had. The contractor believed that all injuries could be prevented. "We are vitally concerned about the human suffering and financial losses resulting from on-the-job accidents, both for the individual and the company," wrote Jerry Morgensen, president of HPCC.[7] For every operation, HPCC conducted an analysis of the hazards and risks associated with that task before it started. And when there was an accident, they intended to discover what had gone wrong and what needed to be done to prevent a recurrence. No exceptions were made to the hard hat, long pants, and work boots rules, even for the many VIPs who would tour the site in the months ahead. Safety training—and communications in general—were provided in English and Spanish, for a large segment of the labor force was from Latin American countries. Safety orientation also gave the Museum an opportunity to let every worker know just how important this project was. They were building "America's Hangar," and it would help preserve aviation and space history for hundreds of years. It wasn't just another building, and everyone got that message.

Hensel Phelps had already studied the

job for many months and had identified the means and methods they would use for constructing the Udvar-Hazy Center. HPCC was going to build from north to south, with one crew dedicated to the mammoth hangar and another to the east wing. But long before footings could be poured or steel put in place, the contractors had to submit plans for how they would transform the architect's drawings into a finished building. As detailed as HOK's drawings and specifications were, they did not include every last nut, bolt, and calculation needed in the field.

HPCC was required to submit multiple copies of "shop drawings" for each submittal category, with all the information needed by the subcontractors to execute each piece of work. HOK's personnel in the field, Tatiana Haggensen and Chet Weber, reviewed the shop drawings or referred them to the architect's consultants. If they approved them, the Smithsonian's construction manager, Vince Cogliano or George Golden, would concur, and then Parsons Brinckerhoff's project administrator, Nicole Ramey, would process the paperwork. If there were questions—and there often were—the paper could get re-routed between the two trailers several times before resolution was achieved. There were enough shop drawings to fill up several file cabinets on both sides of the trailer deck, and they were required for everything, from the flag poles to the information desk to the structural steel. At every weekly owner-contractor progress meeting, the team reviewed the status of submittals and official requests for information (RFI), and there was usually a mad dash just before the

Thursday morning meetings to clear up outstanding issues and fill up one another's in-boxes. By project's end, there were nearly 2,000 written RFIs. Documentation and the management of all that paper was a Herculean task, but in the Smithsonian's trailer Ramey and Katie Marr had it under control.

A circular large-format theater, which would seat about 500, anchored the east wing of the complex on the north end. The 15-by-23-meter (50-by-70-ft) screen would actually extend down below the seating level and far above, giving the audience that special thrill of being part of larger-than-life action and motion. Theaters are never easy to build, and Hensel Phelps was eager to get the pit, down into which the screen would extend, dug and poured. It was one of the first critical tasks on their long to-do list. And from the first day, the theater was plagued by many change orders.

The Smithsonian's Office of Contracting had insisted during the design phase that a specific theater format and vendor should not be specified. This would ensure competition among the small number of vendors in this industry niche and provide best value and price for the Institution. Therefore, HOK could not design a theater for any one specific system; the design was generic. By the time the job was awarded, there was only one system on the market: IMAX®. The National Air and Space Museum had opened on the Mall in 1976 with an IMAX® theater, so the staff was very familiar with the product. However, the technology and dimensions required for IMAX® theaters in 2003 did not match exactly with the design HOK had produced several years earlier. Changes

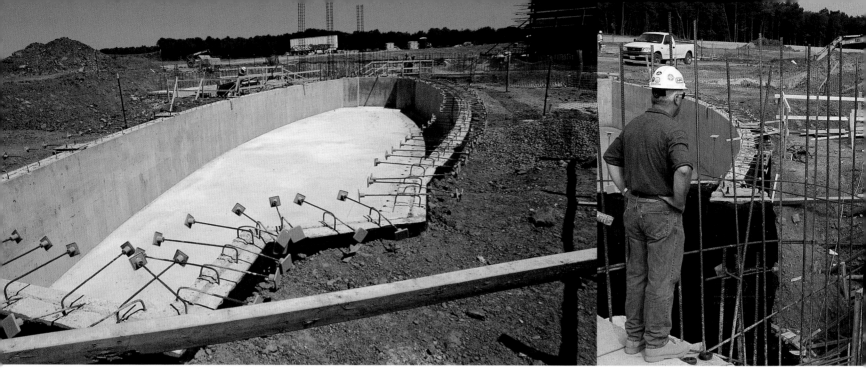

The tall screen of the IMAX® theater required that a pit be dug. The screen would actually extend below the lowest rows of seats.

Crews started assembling the curved theater walls in July 2001, starting on the east and working their way around to the north and west.

were called for in the rake (steepness) of the seating platforms and for several other basic structural and acoustical components. And the vendor could not share the proprietary details of its systems until they had a signed contract with the Smithsonian, something they did not have when Hensel Phelps took to the field. The construction team would modify the theater design details many times, with each change first going through HOK, then to HPCC for shop drawings, then back to HOK for review, and then to the contractor. The folder of revisions for the theater grew to fill its own file cabinet drawer, and the word "theater" usually prompted groans

around work tables in at least two trailers.

Superintendent Rick Lindow named Tony Ball area superintendent for the huge aviation hangar, and his work team also started on the north end of the building. Some 200 aircraft would eventually call this hangar their home, and it was sized accordingly: 75.6 meters (248 ft) wide, 300 meters (984 ft) long, and 31.4 meters (103 ft) tall at its highest point. The 21 large steel arches, which would give the hangar its shape, would each weigh in at 140 tons, with the end trusses being even heavier. Those trusses, spaced a little more than 15 meters

(49 ft) apart, required major support. Laying these foundations was Ball's first task.

HOK's structural engineers had designed triangular bases of steel and concrete to support the weight and loads of the 21 trusses. At each point of the triangle, the base was supported in turn by three caissons, holes dug some 6 to 8 meters (20–25 ft) deep, lined with reinforcing steel rods, and poured full of concrete. A triangular frame was built encasing the three caissons and also filled with concrete. On this base, a steel form was built by ADF, International, Hensel Phelps' steel fabricator. The first steel

was craned into place in June 2001. Using a customized form, the triangular steel structure was then encased in concrete, leaving structure exposed onto which to anchor the steel arches. The end product is known as a thrust block. It took most of the rest of the year to move to the southern end of the hangar, building 21 pairs of thrust blocks. Director Jack Dailey wanted to add to the length of the hangar, and, confident that he could raise the extra $8 million it would take to design and build the additional bays, he had requested and received approval for "alternates 11 and 12." The extra 60 meters (197 ft) brought the total to 21 arches, up from the original 17.

A foundation is precisely engineered to support the size and weight of the structure that will be built or installed on top of it. The foundation is built layer by layer, becoming a sandwich of materials, all closely specified, with the main ingredients being sand, bars of reinforcing steel (called rebar), and concrete. The size of the rebar, provided by Rockingham Steel, and the grid along which it was installed were called out in shop drawings. Concrete pours lasting 7 hours were commonplace for the theater foundation in July 2001. Mountains of rebar were delivered to the site and stored in the parking lot until needed.

Ironworkers spent the winter months erecting the theater's steel frame.

Three caissons were drilled some 6–8 m (20–25 ft) deep into the rock and soil to support the thrust blocks that would form the bases of the giant steel arches of the aviation hangar. Dominion Caisson Corporation went through many auger drill bits chewing up the rock at Dulles during 2001.

R&R Reinforcing, the rebar subcontractor for the entire building, filled each hole with rebar, which was then poured full of concrete. These first caissons were formed in June 2001.

Crews set forms around the steel and poured concrete inside to produce the finished thrust block.

HPCC ordered a second set of forms to speed the assembly line along.

Contractors built a wooden form around the triangle of caissons, forming the basic shape of the thrust blocks, which was also poured in concrete. Rebar extended from each of the caissons.

In June 2001, ADF delivered steel for the first thrust block and craned the members into place. From this experience, an adjustment was made that would speed future installations.

The aviation hangar construction crew also started work on the major east-west utility trench that would take lines of hot and cold water, steam, and other utilities from the central utility plant on the west side of the project to the easternmost part of the building. The job of converting HOK's exacting mechanical and plumbing design to actual pipes, fittings, fixtures, and conditioned space fell to John J. Kirlin, Inc., the mechanical subcontractor. HOK's Dick Powers would visit the site often to assist the contractors with their interpretation of the architects' mechanical design.

By early winter 2001, from the air, the outline of the first phase of the Udvar-Hazy Center was evident. From right to left (east to west): theater, tower stem, and retaining wall of the east wing; double line of thrust blocks for the long aviation hangar; to the southwest is the central utility plant, which houses the chillers, boilers, and other mechanical systems needed to heat and cool the building. Dulles Airport's terminal is four miles north of the construction site, with Runway 1R-19L much closer. To the south of the building footprint, contractors are assembling trusses for the hangar.

Steel on the Horizon

Tony Ball, Area Superintendent, Hensel Phelps Construction Co.

I joined Hensel Phelps in 1989 and came directly from a job at the Pentagon to the Air and Space Museum's project at Dulles. Looking back at the job, what made it especially unique was the close on-site coordination that was required as the Museum moved in its aircraft and spacecraft while we were still finishing the building. That took a lot of trust and communications! But it was the aggressive schedule that really had my attention; we knew up front that the building had to be ready for the December 2003 celebrations.

Our plan for erecting the steel for the aviation hangar was important to the success of the project. We struggled a bit with it in the beginning, but it was a one-of-a-kind process that became increasingly easier as we worked our way from north to south. I'm personally looking forward to being onboard to build the restoration hangar. I want to see this project through to its final conclusion!

One of the issues the technical evaluation team looked at closely when selecting a general contractor for the Udvar-Hazy Center was where the prospective builders would get steel for the job. Most of Hensel Phelps' steel would be made in the United States and fabricated by ADF, International, of Montreal. NASM staff members were especially eager to discuss the installation of the aviation hangar's steel with Hensel Phelps as soon as the contract was let, to explain in greater detail how they would be hanging aircraft from those huge trusses and how important it was that the hangar floor be protected throughout construction. This was "America's Hangar," and it had to look its best. Superintendent Lindow, Steve Speer, and their Hensel Phelps teammates came to the Paul Garber Preservation, Restoration, and Storage Facility in Suitland, Maryland, to meet the Museum's collections team and get a firsthand look at some of the aircraft that would be moved to Dulles. While

the meeting accomplished its objectives—schedules were discussed, expectations explored, hanging methods discussed—the more important outcome was the appreciation that the contractors took away with them that day of what "quality" means to the Air and Space Museum. They observed the meticulous care the restoration team gave to their work; they saw one-of-a-kind artifacts that changed history; they saw the passion the Garber team had for their calling. The owner's expectations of this steel hangar were very high.

The steel trusses of the aviation hangar are triangular in cross section and "architecturally exposed." Visitors will be able to see all the structure in this clear-span hangar; it won't be hidden behind walls and dropped ceilings. No vertical "posts" hold up the roof, and nothing obscures the sight lines of visitors or gets in the way of hanging aircraft. ADF built the monumental trusses using three large curved tubes, or

ADF built customized frames, or jigs, south of where the building would be constructed, onto which to assemble the trusses that would support the aviation hangar.

The first steel for the giant trusses arrived on a flatbed truck in late October. Three curved chords of steel 24 metres (80 ft) long were quickly craned onto the first jig. The trusses are so large that they could be assembled only in thirds: two side pieces and one longer center section for each of the 21 trusses.

On November 14, 2001, a crane operator lifted the first truss section and slowly rotated it to face the aviation hangar. Late that afternoon, the crane walked the 31,750-kilogram (35-ton) steel structure to a thrust block on the northwest side of the hangar where it would be mated with other side sections and lifted into place in the coming weeks. There was plenty of work on this busy site for the crane operators as they relocated truss sections from jigs to temporary storage and finally to the hangar.

Contractors delivered four truss side sections to the west and four to the east on the north end of the hangar, lining them up with their thrust blocks.

chords, of steel, which were fabricated in their Canadian plant and trucked to northern Virginia. Each truss was so big that it could only be delivered, built, and erected in thirds.

Truckers delivered the first three 24-meter (80-ft) chords on a long escorted flatbed in late October. After the tubular steel was craned onto customized jigs, which had been built just north of the construction trailers, ironworkers joined them together using smaller steel members. Project staff had traveled to Canada earlier that month to inspect a mock-up of a completed truss segment. Structural engineers were keen to see the results of a value engineering change proposed by the general contractor, which recommended that the major components of the trusses be bolted together rather than welded. They proved to the owner that labor costs would be lower and that time could be shaved from the schedule. This idea was approved in early June. The Smithsonian's contract encouraged value engineering. NASM had great confidence in HOK's design, but General Dailey challenged the contractors to speak up if they saw ways that the building could be built smarter, faster, or cheaper. Any savings realized as a result of value engineering ideas were to be shared, 55 percent going to the contractor and 45 percent to the Smithsonian. Hensel Phelps, however, pledged to donate all savings to the project and generated a long list of ideas to explore. Bolted connections saved the project $3.7 million.

Hensel Phelps and ADF explored several strategies for assembling the large aviation hangar trusses. Because of their significant size and weight, each truss was assembled on site in three pieces, with two side assemblies each weighing about 31,750 kilograms (35 tons) and one larger 63,500-kilogram (70-ton) center section. With the thrust blocks completed to accept the weight and forces of the trusses, the side sections were lined up with their respective thrust blocks until four were resting in place side by side. In this lowered position, crews began installing galvanized steel deck to the top sides of the trusses, bridging the four into a single unit.

The perforated deck was actually the innermost layer of a sandwich of roofing materials. Three layers of insulating materials came next and finally an outer layer of a flexible membrane roofing material made with Hypalon®. The plan called for all the side-section work to be completed before the structure was lifted into place up on its thrust blocks. It would be safer working at lower altitudes, and the work would go faster. Individual center sections would be dropped in later and the roofing completed up to the peak. The plan would prove to be viable for future blocks of truss sections, but Hensel Phelps was ready in late January 2002 to raise the first sections before all the layers of roofing were in place. Blocks of side sections on the east and west sides on the north end of the hangar were lifted, bolted to thrust blocks, and temporarily shored up on January 28 and 29. On the 30th, the largest crane on the job site slowly moved the first center section into place, and ADF crews grasped the ends. With giant bolts, they made a bridge of steel against the gray winter sky.

Using galvanized steel decking, ADF crews joined four side sections into a single block, but winter weather set in before the first lift could take place.

Two cranes working in tandem lifted the first set of side sections on January 28, 2002. A strong back evenly distributed the weight between the two cranes working on the east side.

Curved guide pins entered center holes of the thrust blocks as the sides were raised. Note the bolted connections. ADF bolted the trusses into place, and the day's work came to an end as the moon rose. The same crews would make the west-side lift in only one hour the next day.

Over the course of the spring, the contractors re-lived this drama many times, and the building's structure marched to completion, north to south, with the last center truss being installed in May.

The first giant 63,500-kilogram (70-ton) center section, 69.5 meters (228 ft) long, was slowly delivered to the north end of the hangar on the afternoon of January 30, 2002, by a 57-meter (188-ft) crane and a very skilled operator. Men clung to safety guidelines as the steel truss moved north. Ironworkers waited, perched on top of the east and west side sections and in nearby boom lifts. At 2:35 p.m., the three men on the west side grasped their end and began the difficult task of fitting the steel into the waiting slots and bolting it together. Just after 3:00, the east team repeated the process. Truss number 68 was complete.

Making the connection.

Steel in high places.

Bob Daniels of Hensel Phelps shows the Steven Udvar-Hazy
family how the aviation hangar is being constructed in April 2002.

At the halfway point, Capitol Sprinkler's staff posted the colors.

On May 30, 2002, the final center truss section was maneuvered into place. Capitol Sprinkler marked the milestone with another American flag, ADF added the Canadian colors, and ironworkers placed the traditional "topping out" tree on the southernmost truss of the aviation hangar.

Site Work, Act 2

Virginia Department of Transportation (VDOT) managers and contractors had the Dulles site mostly to themselves during the first package of site work. The second package would be more challenging and just as important. New Construction, Inc., joined the project as VDOT's second prime contractor in September 2001. Roadways, the parking lot, and the haul road up to the runway had to be completed and the utility installations finished, and, while the job site looked huge from the air, it could seem like close quarters when multiple contractors and deliveries were all coming down the same access road and staging together around the building. Hensel Phelps and New Construction would work literally side by side, as VDOT's contractor completed their work around the perimeter of the building.

There were many issues for VDOT and New Construction to discuss at weekly meetings with Hensel Phelps and the Smithsonian. Many revolved around schedule. When would Contractor A be done with their work in a given space so that Contractor B could proceed? Resolving difficulties fell to VDOT manager Rick Miller and Smithsonian construction managers Cogliano and Golden, all seasoned hands at managing large projects. They juggled priorities and schedules but never compromised on scope of work and quality. In addition to coordinating the contractors' work, which was clearly spelled out, the construction and design managers also dealt with several complex external issues, and the requirements and needs of external parties were not always so apparent. Airport officials were the final authority on issues relating to building codes on the job site, but utilities always came from somewhere else, and those controlling parties all had their own sets of standards, approval processes, and personalities. Design manager David Hay and George Golden shouldered most of the tasks associated with getting the gas, water, sewer, and electrical services properly approved, permitted, paid for, and installed across neighboring properties—so that New Construction could complete their work.

New Construction deposited tons of material to backfill the east retaining wall, as can be seen in this December 2001 aerial photograph—the results of their good work.

Above: By late October, 75 percent of the concrete had been poured for the haul road leading to Runway 1R-19L. That road also serviced both ends of the aviation hangar. The link was complete by spring 2003.

Above right: By late 2003, the 2,000-car parking lot had curbs and light posts and it stood ready and waiting for capacity crowds in December 2003.

Right: New Construction's and Shirley Construction's work on the roadways, parking lots, and interchange was all completed in time for the first appreciation events in early December. The Virginia Department of Transportation dedicated the interchange under an enclosed tent at the height of a sleet storm on December 5, 2003.

The Museum didn't wait for opening day to put the haul road to use!

Rising from the East

By February 2002, all the structural steel for the theater was in place. Steel decks poured with concrete formed the floors and roof of the theater, all in place by March 2003.

As ironworkers and roofing crews were erecting the aviation hangar, other teams were taking the theater and tower to new levels. The east wing was a busy, complex construction site for more than two years, and it would become a dynamic "people space." Visitors to the Udvar-Hazy Center enter the building at the second level and quickly find an important crossroads. Going straight ahead, lured by the sight of aircraft hanging from trusses, they discover the collections. If visitors look right, they will see the theater box office and information desk; to the left, the

museum store and future food court. Nearby stairs and elevators take theatergoers downstairs for a movie. Students may take those same stairs to reach the Claude Moore Education Center with its three classrooms. The Don Engen Observation Tower elevators empty onto both levels. The east wing is designed to hum with activity.

By November 2001, the structural steel for the theater and tower were both going up rapidly. ADF had crews dedicated to these two structures, as well as to the aviation hangar. Materials and supplies for the east

A.C. Dellovade, Inc., installed metal panels to the theater's exterior that reminded the Museum staff of aluminum aircraft skin.

wing were laid out in the cleared parking lot, and cranes steadily fed the supply line with steel beams. Steps seemingly made for giants marched up the interior of the theater. On these concrete landings, seats would be installed. The broad northern wall would serve as a mount for the large screen, and offices and support spaces would run in a concentric circle around the outside of the theater. There would be two projection booths, one for the oversized IMAX® equipment and one for more traditional audio-visual devices. And a rooftop level, complete with terrace, would be "closed in" by Hensel Phelps but left for future development.

With overhead work completed and scaffolding moved out in August 2003, Hensel Phelps moved quickly to install carpeting and seating in the theater. IMAX® had a long list of items they needed to install and test in the projection booth and theater so that the first guests would be treated to the large-screen experience. They needed a completed and very clean space in which to work. Seats and screen complete the picture.

Architect Bill Hellmuth described the entrance area as fuselage-shaped, reminiscent of an aircraft. Although that symbology was hard to appreciate from the ground level, it would be a grand entrance. Overhead, a tall clerestory of windows would help visitors adjust to the lower light levels inside as they walked toward the aviation hangar, by slowly narrowing the stream of light coming in from above.

Below: Striking European ceramic tile, used inside and outside the building along the east-west axis of the structure, was installed by Wyatt, Inc. Depending on the light, the tiles could read marine blue, dark gray, or any shade in between.

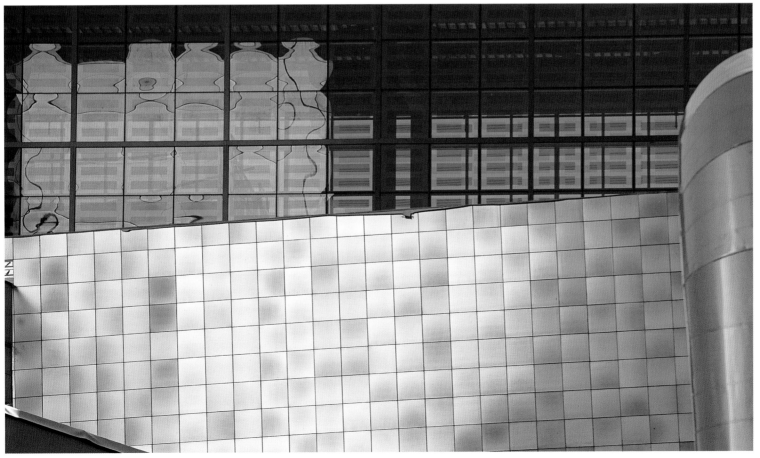

Admiral Don Engen described the 50-meter (164-ft) observation tower as an "architectural icon." The Museum named the tower in honor of NASM Director Engen, who was killed in a glider accident in 1999.

Visitors could look forward to exploring two decks in the cab of the observation tower. They would take an elevator to get there, but that elevator was one of the last items to be completed. Construction crews poured two sets of stairs as part of the tower's stem, or core, and they would walk up and down them many times, carrying equipment and materials to the cab. Large cranes were used to lift the cab's structural steel and glass up the 50-meter (164-ft) tower.

The July 2002 monthly progress report prepared by the Smithsonian noted that the project was at the halfway mark. Days elapsed stood at 457, with 442 left to go. And the Smithsonian had paid out 53 percent of the contract award to Hensel Phelps. At the end of each month, the project team held an executive briefing for managers from the Museum and central Smithsonian offices that had a stake in the project. It was a good opportunity to review progress, schedule, and safety problems and hear about Hensel Phelps' plans for any necessary corrections. Project manager Mark Starkey represented the general contractor, and Vince Cogliano chaired the meetings. The team always went over the change order log and calculated the worth of value engineering savings. Parsons Brinckerhoff's team provided valuable assistance with change orders. They could evaluate the scope and line item costs associated with any proposed changes and helped the construction managers negotiate the best deal for the Smithsonian. And they inspected work constantly as it was completed by the contractors. Paul Dickens of Parsons Brinckerhoff was always on hand for the monthly briefings with insight and good ideas.

Harmon Inc. installed the tinted glass that outlined the ends of the aviation hangar, enclosed the observation tower cab, and graced the front of the building. The panels in the clerestory were made of fritted, or patterned, glass.

The elliptical cab houses two levels, or decks. The top-most is an observation deck, while the second level houses an air traffic control exhibit, guest-curated and funded by the Federal Aviation Administration.

Space Hangar— Launched just in Time

In the spring of 2002, the Air and Space Museum requested approval to proceed with an important option for the Hazy Center. The James McDonnell family had made a generous contribution to the project and specifically asked that their gift be recognized by naming the new home for *Enterprise* and other space artifacts after this aerospace pioneer. Secretary Lawrence M. Small concurred. In April, the Smithsonian exercised its option and directed Hensel Phelps to construct the space hangar and have it

completed for opening day in December 2003. The price was $8,349,000.

The footprint of the second hangar had already been established and the building pad readied by VDOT's contractors. Shop drawings were submitted immediately for the foundation work. HOK had designed a very different structure for the space artifacts; fittingly, it was a spaceframe. The hangar would be open-span, rectangular, and painted dark gray, with a concrete floor thick enough to

support *Enterprise's* weight. Smaller space artifacts would hang from the spaceframe, and just how this would work was the subject of many discussions among the Museum's collections team, structural engineers, Hensel Phelps, and Mero Structures, Inc., the subcontractor who would fabricate and install the spaceframe. Tony Escobar was Hensel Phelps' project engineer for the space hangar.

Fleming Steel donated and installed the hangar doors for the James S. McDonnell Space Hangar.

By late summer, the foundations and most of the substructure that would bear the loads of the structure were in place.

In December 2002, a line-up of Mero's vertical spaceframe columns revealed clues as to the dimensions of the space hangar, which would be 80 meters (262 ft) long, 55 meters (180 ft) wide, and 24 meters (80 ft) tall.

Spaceframe construction went quickly, with Kirlin working in tandem to install the ductwork. The structure was already painted gray, so it would only have to be touched up before artifacts were moved into the space hangar.

After Mero had assembled its frame, crews began applying perforated metal decking in early spring 2003 to top off the space hangar. That job was done by May.

Exterior walls and the sliding hangar doors were clad with metal panels to match the rest of the building. A removable panel for the high tail of *Enterprise* remained open until the shuttle was inside.

Concrete pours for the space hangar began during the summer months of 2003.

Closing up the Building

Mark Starkey, Project Engineer, Hensel Phelps Construction Co.

The Steven F. Udvar-Hazy Center is the most challenging, yet most rewarding, project I have worked on in my 15-year career in construction. The importance of this project in itself made it rewarding. The schedule had to be met to coincide with the 100-year anniversary of the first motorized flight. The quality had to be the best to meet the expectations of being part of the most prestigious Air and Space Museum in the world.

There were many super challenging parts to this project. At the top of the list was the structure. We had one year from notice to proceed on April 23, 2001, to get 5,000 sheets of structural steel shop drawings drafted, engineered, and reviewed, and then fabricate and erect 6.35 million kilograms (7,000 tons) of a very complicated steel structure.

We had a great team on the project, including our staff, owners' representatives, designers, subcontractors, and especially the crafts people who put it all together. The project was completed on time, with excellent quality, minimal injuries, and within the budget. I will always hold this project as one of my life's greatest accomplishments.

Inside the aviation hangar, Hensel Phelps' subcontractors kept to their north-to-south strategy. All the trades had to get into the hangar. ADF had to build a system of mezzanines along the western side and a pedestrian bridge that bisected the hangar, running east-west. A ramp and a stairway would take visitors from a second-level "scenic overlook" down to the hangar floor. And two classy stainless-steel and glass elevators had to be installed by Delaware Elevator, while staircases were wrapped around them. Overhead, exposed supply and return air ducts needed to be hung. Critical sprinkler lines must be installed, hidden among the trusses. Supplying the electrical service was another huge task on the list, and subcontractor MC Dean was also responsible for security systems, IT infrastructure, and audio-visual installations. Speakers for the public address system had to be hung from the highest points of the hangar. All the interior had to be painted white. Monumental overhead braced-arm canopy hangar doors were needed. And finally, the perfect concrete floor had to be poured. And most of this had to be accomplished before the first aircraft could be moved in from the Museum's storage facility.

HOK's lighting designer, Fisher Marantz Stone, called for indirect natural lighting in the aviation hangar, supplemented by electrical lamps. Light from a row of high windows along the east and west sides of the aviation hangar bounced from light shelves up the curvature of the white arched ceiling. A utility catwalk running alongside the light shelves would also serve as a mounting platform for lights. No light fixtures would be installed overhead on the trusses.

In addition to the main utility trench underneath the pedestrian bridge in the aviation hangar, utility trenches for electrical, security, and IT cabling ran the length of the hangar on the east and west sides. MC Dean built large electrical and communications closets along the east and west walls, regularly spaced. Nineteen kilometers (12 miles) of ductwork would run underneath the concrete floors, most of it stretching from closet to closet, east to west, for electrical, security, and data lines. This gave the Museum ultimate flexibility out on the floor of the colossal hangar for exhibitry, mobile lighting towers, or interactive devices that would help visitors appreciate the artifacts displayed there.

In April 2003, the construction team marked the end of the second year in the field. The report for that month tallied the days elapsed at 656, with 246 days left on the adjusted clock. Contractors had logged 1,182,681 staff hours, and 600 workers had contributed to the program. Hensel Phelps had collected 83 percent of the monies due them. After the flurry of value engineering ideas during the first few months, the savings realized had stabilized at $2.36 million, a generous contribution to the building. Cogliano's change order log now carried more than 200 entries. Many of these changes were

chalked up to design deficiencies: details missing in the drawings, miscalculations, omissions, and errors. And many of the deficiencies had been prompted by the quick turnaround demanded of HOK when the Smithsonian elected to further pare back the base building. These change orders amounted to just over 1 percent of the total cost of the building. For a project of this magnitude, 5 percent was the industry standard. Safety had been a hot topic at weekly meetings during the months of steel erection, but a program of vigilance and incentives had turned that around. When compared to national standards, the safety rate for the ironworkers, painters, and masons on the Dulles job was poorer, while mechanical, electrical, and concrete workers, roofers, and carpenters far surpassed safety standards.

It got very busy inside the hangar, as these progress photos demonstrate.

Pouring the Floor for a Black-Tie Hangar

DuBrook Concrete, Inc., brought cement to the Dulles site by truck convoy from a plant only five miles away. Hensel Phelps started the aviation hangar pours early each morning at 4:00 so that the trucks would avoid the region's brutal rush hour traffic. They wanted consistency in the quality of the materials, and time was one contributing factor. Pours started on the north end of the hangar in October 2002 and didn't end on the south end until early March 2003.

When the trucks arrived, operators found a fully prepared zone of the hangar in which their loads of cement would be used. Typically, the largest rectangular area stretched 90 meters (295 ft) in length but was only 6.89 meters (22.6 ft) wide. On the compacted soil, contractors had already applied 15 centimeters (6 in) of number 21A aggregate stone and 10 centimeters (4 in) of number 57 stone, a plastic vapor barrier, 5 centimeters (2 in) of sand, and a maze of

reinforcing bars. Trucks drove into the hangar, which was noisy with the sounds of conveyor belts, running engines, and the voices of scores of workers (most of whom wore oversized rubber boots), all punctuated by the occasional siren signaling a halt to the process. Two trucks were always in the hangar, feeding a conveyor system that guaranteed a steady controlled feed of cement into the form. Over 4½ hours, 22 trucks would deposit their loads.

By October 2002, DuBrook Concrete, Inc., was pouring concrete for the floor at a rate of 2,070 square meters (23,000 sq ft) per week.

Skilled laborers took over after each deposit to smooth the wet material and remove any pockets of air. They waded into the cement with their trowels, bull floats, and vibratory floats, methodically working over every surface so that it was consistently even. Laser screeds ensured that all slabs were precisely poured. The operation was a mix of old-fashioned labor and tools, assisted by modern technology.

A crew from Engineering Consulting Services was on hand in the hangar, too, to test the cement as it came off the trucks. Once every 74 cubic meters (100 cu yds), they took samples to test for the amount of air in the material, its temperature, and its consistency, or slump. Some samples were sent off to a laboratory for compressive strength tests.

Thirty minutes after the pours, the concrete was treated with a shake-on hardener. This silica-based light gray material was supplied by Euclid Chemical Company and applied with a 76-centimeter (30-in) spreader. A belt uniformly shook the material onto the slab, with the edges being treated by hand. To test for a uniform pour, a weight test was performed on a 33-centimeter (1-ft) square every 3 to 4.6 meters (10–15 ft). This process gave the hangar floor its uniform color and sheen. The color extended down through the top layer of the concrete, helping to disguise future minor gouges.

It would take the concrete six to seven hours to set and four days to cure, and Hensel Phelps worked hard to keep the finished slabs covered so that they remained clean and unharmed. But before opening day, almost everyone on the job site would take their turn on the mechanical floor cleaners.

Airport officials had insisted that the Museum's contractor use a specific roofing material. A basic ingredient of the rubber-like roofing membrane that Stevens Roofing Systems uses is Hypalon®, an elastomer made by DuPont Dow Elastomers. The roofing is a scrim-reinforced, heat-weldable, single-ply membrane. After installation, it cures into a more durable cross-linked rubber.

Because of the airport environment, the roof needed to be resistant to chemicals. It could not reflect into the eyes of approaching pilots. And obviously, it had to be flexible to fit the shape of the building and be durable.

Visitors to the construction site marveled at the roofers' skillful application of the rigid insulation and

the Hypalon® outer skin to the building's 72,000-square-meter (800,000-sq-ft) roof. Safety equipment for the Pioneer Roofing crew included full body harness. By late fall 2002, Pioneer had installed some 25,920 square meters (288,000 sq ft) of roofing material.

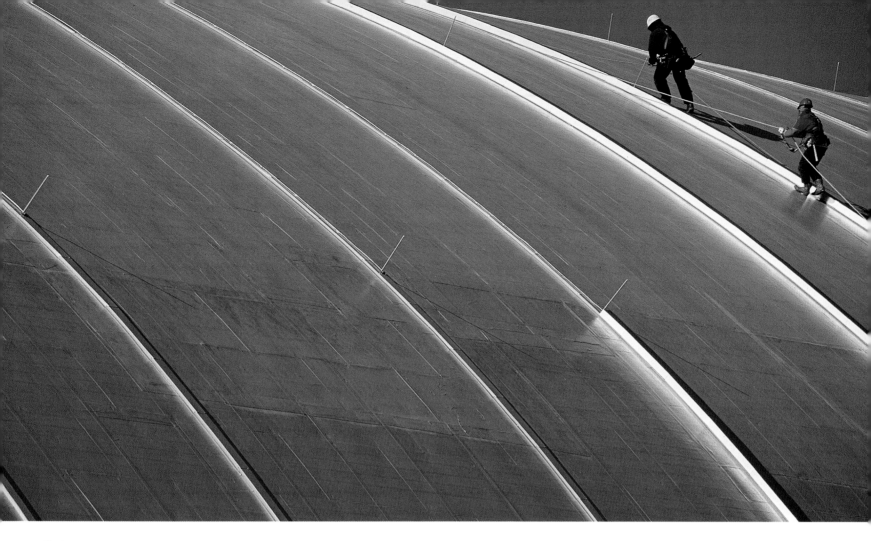

The innermost layer of the aviation hangar's ceiling-to-roof sandwich is perforated steel deck. Not all the decking could be applied before the trusses were fully erected. Deck over the center sections was applied in place, and what a view!

Two layers of rigid insulation were applied to the steel deck, topped off by the flexible membrane roof, which Pioneer Roofing crews unrolled down the hangar.

It took nine months to install 27 kilometers (17 miles) of 1.8-meter-(6-ft) wide membrane to the roof of the Udvar-Hazy Center. An average of 30 people worked on the crew at any one time.

The end trusses were strengthened to carry the extra weight and loads of the hangar doors. Fleming Steel of New Castle, Pennsylvania, provided the overhead braced arm canopy doors, which met the Museum's strict requirements. Either half could open independently. A small "doggy door" on either end is actually big enough for a tractor trailer. This system would give the Museum the option of opening only as much door as it needed, and the Museum certainly needed to open the door all the way when the Concorde and the Dash-80 came to Dulles to stay.

Finishing up Inside

Painting the high levels of the aviation hangar required a flotilla of lifts. Glidewell Brothers, Inc., had to reach up to the top of this 31.4-meter (103-ft) home for historic aircraft and in between every nook and cranny, and it took 26,880 liters (7,100 gallons) of white paint!

Interior walls were finished by Dulles Drywall. There are several grades of drywall finish, and HOK specified a high-end finish for all the public spaces, which required multiple passes with sanding equipment and great attention to detail.

Capitol Sprinkler workers took great pride in hiding their work, but the Museum took comfort in knowing that the collections would be protected in the event of fire. Installation was only half the story; Capitol had to test the system, too.

In mid-March 2003, the National Air and Space Museum was given beneficial occupancy of the aviation hangar so that it could begin the task of moving aircraft in from their storage hangars. Hensel Phelps had many tasks left in the hangar. Record-breaking snow and ice that winter had damaged exterior ductwork and mechanical-electrical rooms outside the hangar, so temporary heaters had to be rented. Not all the electrical service was live yet; there wasn't any potable water; there was a steady stream of construction workers in the hangar. But the Museum was happy to be moving in, even if it meant camping out and getting imaginative. By May, 50 artifacts were under roof.

Predictably, hundreds of little problems started showing up on a running list of things to do to finish the job during the final months. The construction trades call it a "punchlist." Owner and general contractor alike want to bring any job to a successful and on-time conclusion. At the Udvar-Hazy Center, this was especially true since thousands of visitors were expected for opening events in mid-December. And it was all the more difficult to achieve since the Museum was moving in, installing IT systems, setting up exhibits, and trying to settle into some routine of doing business at Dulles. Inevitably, but not often, owner and contractor got in one another's way. It became difficult to account for who had just nicked the wall that had been painted the day before, or which trade had just damaged the work of another. Although NASM tried to protect its installed aircraft and spacecraft with sheets of plastic—even those hanging 12 m (40 feet) off the floor—the staff was rightly concerned about construction dust and debris, which made the contractors' work harder.

Wooden acoustical tiles were a classy touch, and they helped absorb noise in the busy entranceway.

During the last months of construction, Tony Ball assigned teams to punchlist duty, led by area superintendent Mark Marcot, who compared lists almost daily with the Smithsonian and with Parsons Brinckerhoff staff, who were conducting detailed inspections for the Smithsonian. Building manager Rick Cochran and his building services contractor team, Consolidated Engineering Services, Inc. (CES), also played an important role during the punchlist and building start-up period. They helped document the condition of the building they would be responsible for operating and learned from the mechanical, electrical, and plumbing subcontractors how to run the physical plant. Long after opening day, the Smithsonian field team and Hensel Phelps struggled to bring all the building's automated systems on line, balance the air handlers throughout the big building, and keep everything running while thousands of visitors came for their first look at the new facility. Everyone expected the job to be tough, and the team had prepared well.

From the Field

Vincent T. Cogliano, PE, Resident Engineer, Smithsonian Institution

As the Resident Engineer, or owner's representative, for the project (as well as the Assistant Administrative Contracting Officer), I was in the unique position of overseeing and managing the administrative processes and daily flow of all issues and nuances that occurred during the project's period of performance. From the start, we tried to establish a true partnering agreement among our many contributing parts: the general contractor, the architect engineer, the Virginia Department of Transportation, which constructed most of the site work for us, the construction management firm, the users (the National Air and Space Museum and Smithsonian Business Ventures) and the Metropolitan Washington Airports Authority, the actual owner of the property and code authority. I am most proud of the way these separate entities really stepped up and worked together to achieve the project's success. I believe that the excitement and unique characteristics of the project itself gave the team the impetus and momentum we needed to carry us through to the end.

The project began six months later than expected but our milestone for opening on December 15th never changed. One challenge was to strive for a submittal review time of seven days. HOK was tremendous in helping us. We also devised a method to provide concise clear direction to the general contractor through the Request for Information process to confirm directions and supplemental instructions, thereby minimizing the letter-writing that sometimes results in bunker mentalities. The results: an extremely low change order rate and zero delay claims.

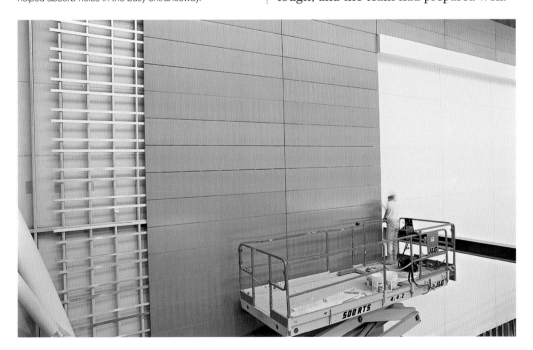

Supporting it All

The design of the Route 28 interchange had been completed in 2001, but VDOT did not announce the job until early 2002. Prospective contractors were shown the site in February, but because the Commonwealth's funding for this highway improvement was bound to a larger program of work, which was being performed by a public-private partnership, construction could not commence until that partnership had been approved. VDOT gave Shirley Construction Company the notice to proceed in June 2002. A partial interchange would be ready in time for opening day, with the full interchange completion date scheduled for spring 2004. The partial interchange would be sufficient for the Center, but the full interchange would be needed when the land on the east side of the highway was developed. The interchange would lead visitors to Air and Space Museum Parkway.

A porte cochere, a high-tech covered porch, protected visitors "de-planing" at the front door. Mero Structures provided the spaceframe for this architectural accent as well as the structure for the space hangar.

In addition to the central utility plant with its boilers and chillers, John J. Kirlin, the mechanical systems subcontractor, installed air handlers outside the building, sized to condition the air of a specific zone. Large-diameter ducts connected the air handlers to the building, all in locations that are not usually visible by the public.

By late summer 2003, boilers, chillers, and air handlers were being tested and run.

John Safer's sculpture *Ascent* was installed in front of the building on a warm summer-like day in September 2003 by Tallix, the foundry that formed and delivered it in two pieces. Assembly took all day, followed by a day of polishing. HOK worked with Safer to design a base that incorporated a fountain, lined with a "streambed" of carefully positioned stones.

Spring planting season brought with it cherry, pin oak, green ash, red maple, white oak, willow oak, and berry trees, adding to the pallet of evergreens that had wintered over along the roadways and parking lots. Photo by Caroline Sheen.

The National Air and Space Society manages the National Aviation and Space Exploration Wall of Honor program. HOK designed the stainless-steel panels that line the walkway to the front door of the Udvar-Hazy Center. For more information, log on to the Museum's web site at http://www.nasm.si.edu/getinvolved.

Construction Statistics from Hensel Phelps

22,222 cubic meters (30,000 cu yds) of excavation

29,630 cubic meters (40,000 cu yds) of concrete

5.9 million kilograms (6,500 tons) of steel

7,830 square meters (87,000 sq ft) of masonry

72,000 square meters (800,000 sq ft) of roofing

45 kilometers (28 miles) of roofing seams

39,000 pieces of roofing insulation

18,810 square meters (209,000 sq ft) of metal panels

10 elevators

18 sets of stairs

19 kilometers (12 miles) of Walker duct for cabling

26,880 liters (7,100 gallons) of white paint for aviation hangar

Aerial progress photographs

September 2001

November 2001

March 2002

April 2002

Each month, usually during the first or second week as weather permitted, Hensel Phelps' photographer took aerial progress photographs from at least two vantage points. In this series, the photographer was aiming southwest. Photographs in this sequence range from September 2001 to December 2003. It is clear that construction crews started on the north end and worked their way south. The space hangar, which was not part of the base building, is not visible until February 2003, but if you look closely at the August 2002 image, you can see the first white concrete footers start to mark the outline.

December 2001

January 2002

June 2002

August 2002

September 2002

December 2002

April 2003

July 2003

February 2003

March 2003

October 2003

December 2003

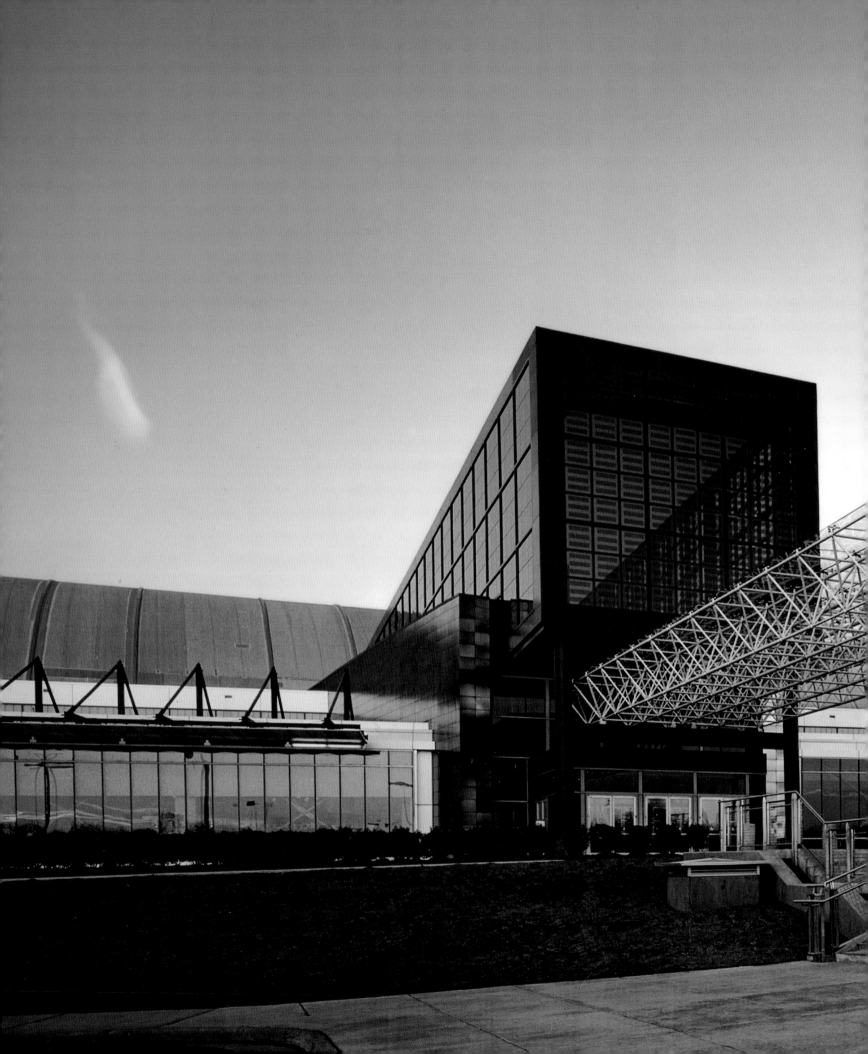

CHAPTER FIVE

Moving in and Starting up

THE NATIONAL AIR AND SPACE MUSEUM STARTED MOVING ARTIFACTS INTO THE STEVEN F. UDVAR-HAZY CENTER ON ST. PATRICK'S DAY IN 2003, WHILE HENSEL PHELPS WAS STILL FINISHING THE HANGAR. IT WAS A DYNAMIC EXERCISE IN PLANNING, COOPERATION, AND TEAMWORK, WITH SOME LUCK THROWN IN. OUR FRIENDS, SUPPORTERS, POTENTIAL SUPPORTERS, AND COLLEAGUES LOOKED IN ON THE MOVE-IN OPERATION OFTEN, AND THERE WAS A CRESCENDO OF INTEREST AS WE APPROACHED THE DECEMBER OPENING DAY. COLLECTIONS AND EXHIBITS STAFF, CURATORS, AND HELPERS LOADED AND UNLOADED TRUCKS. THEY PUT THE AIRCRAFT BACK TOGETHER, HUNG THEM IF THAT WAS IN THE PLANS, AND READIED THEM FOR EXHIBITION.

Joe Anderson, Jack Dailey, and Don Lopez cut the ribbon.

Piper J-3 Cub.

Above: Director Jack Dailey (right) and Steven F. Udvar-Hazy (left).

Right: Smithsonian Secretary Lawrence M. Small, NASM Director Dailey, and Steve Hazy toast the opening of the Center.

Smithsonian
National Air and Space Museum
Steven F. Udvar-Hazy Center

In early November, the team said it was time to unwrap the treasures and get ready for company. Enjoy this scrapbook of memories and consult Appendix 4 for a complete list of aircraft and spacecraft that were moved in for opening day. And see Appendix 5 for details on the exhibits team and the components of the lighting system for the building and the exhibitions. The Museum's web site at http://www.nasm.si.edu can give you the latest information on additions as staff continue to relocate artifacts to the Udvar-Hazy Center.

NAF N3N-3 *Yellow Peril*

Exhibit stations

On opening day, these 10 exhibit stations helped guide visitors through the artifacts on dispay:

Pre-1920 Aviation

Business Aviation

Sport Aviation

General Aviation

Commercial Aviation

World War II Aviation

Cold War Aviation

Korea and Vietnam

Modern Military Aviation

Reaching into Space

Artifact cases throughout the facility displayed objects that covered the following themes:

Aerial Cameras

Aerobatic Flight

Aircraft Machine Guns

Aircraft Propulsion

Airliner Models

Astronaut Equipment

Balloonamania

Bell No. 2 Rocket Belt

Lt. Gen. James H. Doolittle's Uniform

Naval aviator Donald D. Engen

Charles A. Lindbergh

Amelia Earhart

Evolution of the Helicopter

General Aviation Aircraft Models

General Henry H. "Hap" Arnold

MiG-15 Pilot's Flight Suit

Roscoe Turner

Royal Canadian Squadron Uniform

SR-71 and RF-4 Pilots' Suits

U.S. Air Force F-16 Pilot Flight Suit

Women in Military Aviation

America's Hangar

Boeing B-29 Superfortress *Enola Gay*

Lockheed SR-71 Blackbird

Space Shuttle *Enterprise*

Boeing 367-80

Concorde

Boeing 307 Stratoliner

Vought F4U-1D Corsair

Curtiss P-40E Warhawk

De Havilland-Canada D.H.C.1 Chipmunk

Monocoupe 110 Special *Little Butch*

Students gather around a century of aviation history. This mural was donated to the Udvar-Hazy Center by aviation and space artist Robert McCall and NASA Dryden Research Center.

Jake Jacobs designed this barrier system to corral groups of artifacts together throughout the large aviation hangar. The exhibit system, which incorporated components for thematic graphics, identifying labels, audio-visual devices, interactive exhibits, seating, and lighting, was first prototyped at the National Air and Space Museum in Washington, D.C. Improvements were made, and Design & Production, Inc., produced the units under contract to the Museum. These exhibit stations introduce visitors to the themes represented by the featured artifacts, while standardized individual labels discuss the specific aircraft and spacecraft. Three types of cases were also designed for smaller artifacts. Large storefront cases were built to exacting standards by Helmut Guenschel, Inc. Other cases used throughout the Center were provided by Crystalizations Systems, Inc., and include special features to provide a stable environment and enhanced security for the valuable contents. And volunteer docents add a personal touch as they lead visitors through the treasures of flight.

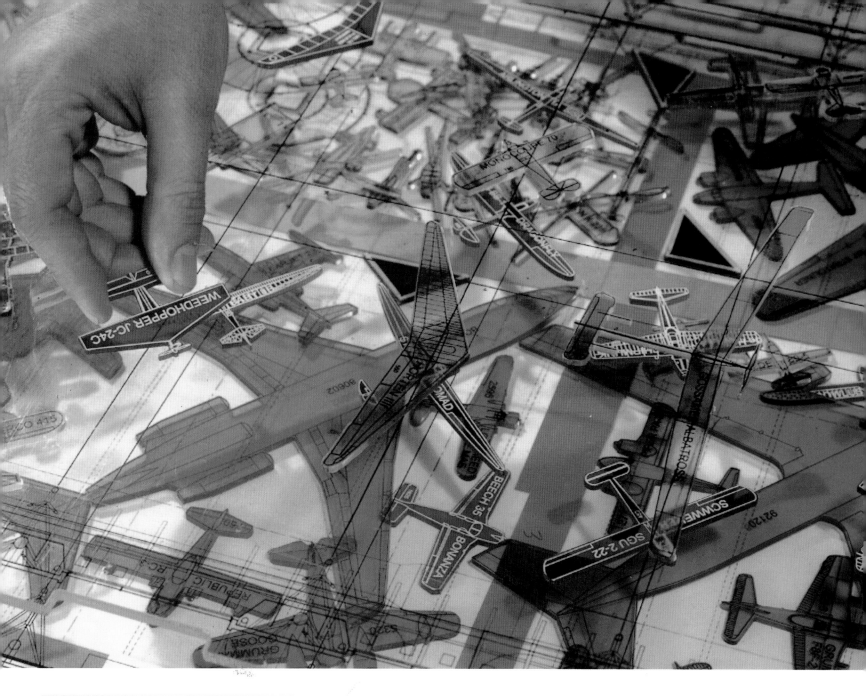

National Air and Space Museum staff worked together to determine just how many aircraft and spacecraft could be installed at the Udvar-Hazy Center. Curators, collections personnel, and exhibits designers graduated from cardboard cutouts to a very accurate and large tabletop plex model with multiple levels onto which plex cutouts of the artifacts were moved around until everyone was satisfied that all areas of the collection were well represented. Curators Russ Lee and Dorothy Cochrane study the aviation hangar model, as exhibit designer William "Jake" Jacobs uses a three-dimensional computer-assisted drawing program to record the latest positions of aircraft in the hangar. Jacobs used a CADDMicrosystems product for this task, and the results were so accurate that the nose of the largest aircraft could be counted on to land within an inch or two of a taped red "X" on the hangar floor during move-in. The 3-D program also allowed the planners to avoid any conflicts among artifacts hanging at several altitudes and in various angles of attack.

The Magic of Light

Lighting designers for the aviation hangar developed two concepts: give the large volume of the hangar a presence and give the planes the feeling of being in flight. Hellmuth, Obata + Kassabaum's lighting designers, Fisher Marantz Stone, provided the first part, and the Museum's exhibition lighting designer, Frank A. Florentine, FIES, LC, supplied the second.

Paul Marantz and Scott Hershman reflected light off the ceiling from a light shelf approximately 15 meters (50 ft) off the floor, bouncing light up the arc of the great hangar's white ceiling. Critical elements to the success of this approach were high-wattage metal halide light fixtures, precise beam patterns, and the reflectance values of the finished ceiling. The target design standard was to provide 200 lux (20 footcandles) at the floor.

Frank Florentine installed light fixtures in various positions throughout the aviation hangar: from knee-high fixtures incorporated into the exhibit barrier system to 7.5-meter (25-ft) RibbonLifts to 10-meter (33-ft) lights mounted on top of electrical closets. Together, they contributed to giving the planes a sense of motion. A variety of light fixtures utilizing metal halide lamps brighten the spaces under, over, and around the artifacts, while filling the shadows with energy.

Long before opening, a television producer paid a visit to start planning his coverage of opening day. When he first visited the hangar, not all the lighting systems were on line, and he predicted that many additional lights would be needed before the huge space was adequately lit. Upon returning to the Center after sections of the hanger were completely lit with artifacts in place, he simply stood in awe and said, "Wow!" Florentine reports: "Lights do that."

Opening day visitors enjoy the collections.

Where to Sit?

Obviously, the focus of the Museum is on preserving its valuable collections of artifacts and providing the public access to them. But staff and visitors alike need a place to sit—especially after walking the length of the hangar a few times—and an efficient place to work. Visitors will find public benches and seating throughout the facility that is in keeping with the bold look of the building. But what about behind the scenes?

HOK designed the administrative offices of the Udvar-Hazy Center to be efficient and flexible. There is a sense of design continuity as one walks from public spaces to private offices and workstations. Materials, upholstery, and finishes were selected to complement the hues and textures of the aircraft on display. Anodized aluminum was used on all pieces where metal was exposed, to mimic materials found on many an aircraft nearby.

Hellmuth, Obata + Kassabaum provided the Museum with an overall design philosophy for the Center's furnishings. Washington Workplace, the furnishings contractor, followed their general design as they selected products for all areas of the building. The Museum was especially eager to get good value. Their team included: Christine Miller Langemak, Vice President; Clifton Cheatham, Design Director; Katie Grauman,

Project Manager; and Fred and Bob Elliott, of Metro Services for installation.

Cheatham designed the workstations and private offices to work together seamlessly by using the same manufacturer, Affordable Interior Systems, for both areas. The furnishings layouts blend well, incorporating the same finishes and the same functional elements, such as flipper door cabinets, open shelves, and personal wardrobe towers. Glass was used in tall workstation panels to allow natural light from nearby window walls to get in, yet keep privacy intact. Open framed panels allowed for ease of access to in-wall power and data connections. Affordable Interior Systems offered an affordable price point without sacrificing durability.

Washington Workplace selected SitOnIt Seating as the primary seating manufacturer, in part because of the lifetime warranty and price this manufacturer provided. They offered multiple styles within one family of chairs so that there was an easy transition between special-use pieces and general seating products.

A few areas of the Center demanded special attention. The Director's conference room and the theater's "green room" were furnished with Krug's Virtu line. It sets these rooms in a modern tone,

using cherry, aluminum trim, and dark toned leather.

Designer Cheatham studied many materials available on the market to find those that provided extra features required by the Museum. For the laboratory-style classroom chairs, he specified a woven crypton from ArcCom, which can be cleaned with a bleach solution, and the laminate for the work tables can withstand spills from future astronauts.

Washington Workplace partnered with Metro Services for the installation of thirteen tractor trailers filled with furniture, which arrived at the site over a three-week period. And the furniture came in the same way the aircraft did, through the hangar doors. A crew of sixteen people worked three weeks non-stop to ensure that everything was in place for opening day, usually working around and beside the general contractor and the Museum's staff.

"A project like this is a dream come true for someone who grew up in the Metro area. I visited the National Air and Space Museum each year on field trips from 3rd through 8th grades," remembers Washington Workplace's Christine Miller Langemak. "I am so excited to be a part of a museum that will bring joy to a new generation of children, which will include my own."

Museum staff based at the Udvar-Hazy Center have a good place to work—for many reasons, including the furniture.

Builders of America's Hangar

About the Photographers

Construction of the Steven F. Udvar-Hazy Center was blessed with intense photographic documentation. Some of it was required by the Smithsonian's contract with Hensel Phelps. Other valuable archives of photos were captured by members of the construction team who were on site every day. And the Smithsonian's professional photographers were regularly called on to record milestone events, take progress photos, and record the installation of artifacts. There must not be a square inch of the site and building left unphotographed. The result: thousands of images in a variety of formats and resolutions, an embarrassment of riches with which to illustrate the story of building America's hangar.

Digital photography was of great value during this project for a variety of purposes. Photos taken by the field team were often quickly shared as e-mail attachments with colleagues and consultants at other locations, who used the images to help solve problems and answer questions. The author regularly took digital photos for staff members responsible for raising funds, who could then send images that were only hours old to donors and prospective donors. Everyone's digital images could easily be added to the Museum's web site or inserted into progress reports. It was a naturally photogenic project, and we made good use of the many images we captured.

Photographs can tell some technical stories more easily than words, and we have used them generously to walk the reader through some of the building processes and construction steps that led to the completion of a truly marvelous building. And we invited the photographers to send us their best and their most artistic work. The hard part was deciding what we could use in just one volume.

Throughout this book, we have not matched up images and photographers with specific credit lines. When we used a photograph by someone other than the talented people we are introducing you to on these pages, we made a note of that photographer's name.

Mark Avino

Mark Avino

Mark Avino has been the chief photographer for the National Air and Space Museum since 1983. He is a graduate of Rochester Institute of Technology. His photography has been featured in countless publications of the Smithsonian, including *At the Controls, the Smithsonian National Air and Space Museum Book of Cockpits* and *America's Smithsonian*. Mark is regularly requested, often with little notice, to photograph events, people, and historic activities taking place at the Museum. Mark primarily used Nikon equipment and Nikor lenses for the Udvar-Hazy shoots, as well as multiple layers of clothing to ward off the winter wind that blows nonstop at Dulles. Mark recalls, too, the bright yellow boots the contractors provided

him for those extra muddy days. He said that "It's been fun shooting the construction of the Hazy Center and the Engen Tower. It reminded me of my summer jobs I worked during college breaks for the construction company in my home town in upstate New York." In recalling the project, Mark remembered one day especially, September 14, 2001: "It was a gloomy morning after the terrible occurrences of the 11th. I was watching the memorial services at the National Cathedral on TV. When it was over, the blue sky broke out so I ran to the window from my office, grabbed my camera bag, and headed out to Dulles. It was so quiet out there, even the sky was without a single airplane flying. All of the workers had been sent home due to the heavy rain earlier in the morning. I was alone at the site to see if I would be able to capture any of the structures with the beautiful clouds in the background. It was so peaceful at the Engen Tower, as if the late Don Engen was up there with his arms wide open for all those who perished at the World Trade Center and the Pentagon."

Duane Lempke

Sisson Studios Inc. was Hensel Phelps' official project photographer. Hensel Phelps' contract with the Smithsonian called for monthly progress photos of every aspect of their work, including aerial photographs. Duane Lempke, after retiring as a Colonel from the U.S. Army in 1993, pursued a degree in photography and joined the staff of Sisson Studios. Since then, he has specialized in construction progress, architectural, aerial, and commercial photography. A native of Kewanee,

Illinois, Duane's photos have been featured on magazine covers, in other books, and in exhibitions. He has logged in more than 150 hours in helicopters taking aerial shots. Sisson assigned him the job of recording the Udvar-Hazy Center's progress toward completion. When asked about the Air and Space Museum's project at Dulles, he said, "It was never easy getting into Dulles airspace. After using three helicopter companies, three types of choppers, once a month for 27 months, it took two hours of preparation per flight to get 10 minutes of aerial images. With the tower's permission, we would slip in between the two major Dulles North/South runways and circle the site, holding our altitude at 700 feet and keeping our distance from landing international and domestic flights. The results: a bird's-eye view of historical proportions."

Duane Lempke

Eric F. Long

Senior photographer Eric Long has been with the Smithsonian's Office of Photographic Services since 1983. Currently assigned to the National Air and Space Museum, his responsibilities include documenting the collections of air and space artifacts, photographing exhibitions and events, and contributing to publications and research. Eric has participated in the historical photo documentation of three Presidential inaugurals and the 100th anniversary of powered flight. His work has been published in *Air and Space Magazine* and was featured in the books *On Miniature Wings, Star Wars—The Magic of Myth*, and *At the Controls*, among others. He has also been an instructor for the National Park Service, teaching documentary photography in Native American communities. His gentle humor and extraordinary talents are widely recognized and appreciated at the Smithsonian.

Eric F. Long

R. Craig Parham

R. Craig Parham

Capitol Sprinkler Contracting, Inc., sent Craig Parham, senior vice president, to the Udvar-Hazy project as part of the team responsible for installing the sophisticated fire protection systems required for the building. The Museum got a bonus, however, because Craig also photographed the project extensively—and from some unique vantage points. He could regularly be seen high up on lifts and rooftops, not just inspecting his crew's work but also taking some great photographs. Craig helped the other photographers gain access to the project by lending them ladders and teaching them not to fear heights. When the aircraft and spacecraft started arriving, he was just as enthusiastic about that subject matter. And he could often be found on the job very early or very late to capture Dulles sunrises and sunsets over the new Center.

Dane Penland

Dane Penland has been a Smithsonian photographer for the Office of Photographic Services since 1977. During his long career, his assignments have exposed him to the riches and diversity of the Institution's collections. Dane has photographed marine biology specimens, the gem collection, rare musical instruments, militaria, people, and places. He literally made the switch from shooting gems to shooting aircraft during the move-in at the Udvar-Hazy Center within one week. He loves what he does at the Smithsonian because he is constantly learning about something new. His favorite projects: gem collection photography and his series of posters featuring musical instruments. When he's not behind the camera lens or at the computer managing the many images he takes, he works with his wife at one of two companies they have been running for the past eight years: a web site development firm and an on-line invitation and registration company. He lives with wife and daughter in Reston, Virginia.

Dane Penland

Carolyn Russo

Since 1988, Carolyn Russo has been a staff photographer at the National Air and Space Museum. She received her B.F.A. in photography from the Massachusetts College of Art and has exhibited her work in solo and group shows nationally. She is the author of two books, *Artifacts of Flight* and *Women and Flight: Portraits of Contemporary Women Pilots*. A widely circulated Smithsonian Institution Traveling Exhibition Services exhibit also featured Carolyn's work from *Women and Flight*. She lives in Virginia

Carolyn Russo

with her husband and two children and is currently working on her third book. From the day the first trees came down at the Udvar-Hazy site, Carolyn could be counted on to travel to Dulles and photograph the progress. Her images of the people who worked on the project are especially valued by the author.

Jeff Pulford and Mark Burlison

Museum staff were introduced to Interface Multimedia through Hellmuth, Obata + Kassabaum (HOK), the architects of the Steven F. Udvar-Hazy Center. Jeff Pulford and Mark Burlison, who founded the company in 1993, aren't project photographers like the other people on these pages, but they did help inspire the staff and its supporters by giving us "virtual" photographs of the facility before there was anything there to photograph. The National Air and Space Museum used Interface Multimedia's images to inspire donors to pledge their support of the project, often customizing a view to meet the Museum's specific needs of the moment. And the computer

Above: The photographers lived the project alongside the construction and move-in teams, always on hand for the milestone shots and the dramatic images, such as this one, featuring the SR-71 and *Enterprise*.

Below: "Virtual" photography was provided by the architects long before there were aircraft hanging at Dulles.

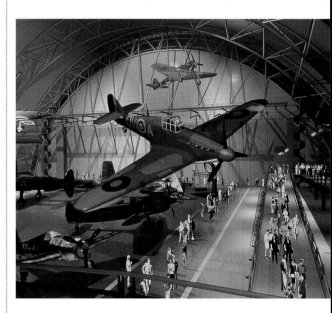

renderings assisted the staff in visualizing details of the design that were difficult for non-architects to understand. Using HOK's three-dimensional computer drawings and the specifications, these talented artists added depth, color, and personality to the files—even artifacts, exhibits, and people.

Contract Team for Building the Steven F. Udvar-Hazy Center

Under the guidance of general contractor Hensel Phelps Construction Co., the following subcontractors and vendors contributed special expertise to building the Steven F. Udvar-Hazy Center:

A. C. Dellovade, Inc.
Profiled metal wall panels and insulated metal wall panels

ADF International, Inc.
Steelwork and miscellaneous metals

Air Power, Inc.
Blasting

All-VA-State Pest Control
Termite control

American Amplifier
Public address and audio-visual systems

Arden Architectural Specialties, Inc.
Impact resistant wall protection

Berkel & Company Contractors, Inc.
Rock anchors

Bettinger West Interior Inc.
Access floor

BFPE International
Fire extinguishers and cabinets (materials only)

Brunswick Woodworking
Architectural woodwork, wood paneling, and cast resin countertop systems

Bunting Graphics, Inc.
Graphics, signage

C&T Equipment Co., Inc.
Paint spray booths

Calvert Masonry, Inc.
Masonry

Capitol Sprinkler Contracting, Inc.
Fire protection

Cedar Run Contracting
Structural foundation backfill

Cooper Material Handling, Inc.
Metal lockers

CPI International
Translucent walkway cover

Curtis Equipment, Inc.
Food service

Davenport (Cary Corporation)
Sprayed-on fireproofing

David Allen Company
Tile and terrazzo

Delaware Elevator
Elevators

Delta Graphics Inc.
Folding and portable stages

Dominion Caisson Corporation
Caissons

DuBrook Concrete, Inc.
Concrete (material only)

Dulles Drywall, Inc.
Drywall and acoustic panels

Engineering Consulting Services, Inc.
Testing and inspection

Environmental Interiors, Inc.
Stainless-steel panels, formed metal base, and perforated metal panels

Fibergate Composite Structures Inc.
Fiberglass grating (materials only)

Firvida Construction Co.
Stonework

Fleming Steel Company
Hangar doors

Flippo Construction Co., Inc.
Site storm drainage

Frank J. Dean Co. Inc.
Acoustic isolation systems

Gallagher & Stone, Inc.
Lab casework

Glidewell Brothers, Inc.
Painting, vinyl wallcovering, and intumescent coating systems

H2OBBS Architectural Fountains
Fountain (mechanical and electrical)

C. H. Edwards
Door hardware and frames

Harmon Inc.
Curtain wall and glazing

Industrial Floor Corporation
Seamless epoxy floor

Interlock Paving, Inc.
Unit pavers

ISEC Corporation Services
Cold room

Jack Bays, Inc.
Metal building systems

John J. Kirlin, Inc.
Mechanical contractor

Kalwall Corporation
Translucent wall panel system

Kewaunee Scientific Corp.
Laboratory casework and fixtures

Long Fence Co., Inc.
Gates and ornamental fence

Loral Concrete
Concrete place and finish (slabs only)

Material Distributors Inc.
Miscellaneous materials, such as flagpoles, mirror units, and tack boards

MC Dean
Electrical contractor

Mero Structures, Inc.
Steel space frame systems

Metal Sales & Services, Inc.
Composite and perforated aluminum panels and metal column covers

Modern Doors & Equipment Sales Inc.
Operable panel and accordion folding partitions

Nystrom Building Products
Expansion joint covers and floor access doors

Overhead Door Company of Washington DC
Overhead doors and dock equipment

Parking Booth Company Inc.
Prefabricated toll booths

Patton Harris Rust & Associates, pc
Surveyor

Pessoa Construction Co.
Site concrete

Pioneer Roofing, Inc.
Roofing, roof hatches, and roof covers

Pollock & Guy Associates Inc.
Metal louvers (material only)

Pro-Bel Enterprises Limited
Window washing equipment

Prospect Waterproofing Company
Waterproofing

R&R Reinforcing
Reinforcing steel installation

RE:Source Washington DC
Resilient tile, sheet vinyl, carpet, and base materials

Rockingham Steel
Reinforcing steel supply

Safety Storage Inc.
Hazardous materials storage lockers (material only)

Seward Hoist & Crane Systems, Inc.
Hoists and cranes

Sisson Studios
Project photography, including aerial photography

Spacesaver Systems Inc.
High-density movable shelving systems
and metal shelving

Sun Control Systems
Window shades

Supersky Products, Inc.
Metal framed skylight

Time & Parking Control
Parking control equipment

Tru-Green Land Care LLP
Landscaping

Valley Crane and Rigging Inc.
Hazardous materials storage lockers (install only)

Victor Stanley Inc.
Site furniture

Wyatt, Inc.
Composite tile panels

Under the guidance of architectural firm Hellmuth, Obata + Kassabaum, Inc., the following subcontractors and vendors played key roles in designing and building the Steven F. Udvar-Hazy Center:

Construction Cost Inc.
Cost estimator

Dames & Moore
Environmental consultant

Erbschloe Consulting Services, Inc.
Builder's hardware

Fisher Marantz Stone
Lighting design

Gage Babcock & Associates
Security and fire protection

Hellmuth, Obata + Kassabaum, Inc.
Mechanical-electrical-plumbing engineer

Interface Multimedia, Inc.
3-D computer visualizations and animated visualizations

Law Engineering
Geo-technical

Patton Harris Rust & Associates, pc
Civil engineer

Robert L. Seymour & Associates
Elevator consultant

Shen Milsom & Wilke, Inc.
Acoustical, audiovisual, and information technology

Spiegel Zamecnik & Shah, Inc.
Structural engineering

URS Corp.
Wetlands design

Other contractors who were a part of the Udvar-Hazy Center team include:

Parsons Brinckerhoff Construction Services, Inc.
Construction management

Cherry Hill Construction Co.
Prime contractor, site preparation, package 1, VDOT

Air Power, Inc.
Blasting

The Brothers Signal Co.
Electrical utilities

Gull Corporation
Box culvert construction

C. C. Johnson Co.
Clearing and grubbing

Locust Lane Farms, Inc.
Grass seeding

Long Fence Co., Inc.
Fencing

Ridge Limited
Environmental controls

Virginia Erosion Control
Environmental controls

Virginia Paving Co.
Asphalt paving

New Construction, Inc.
Prime contractor, site preparation, package 2, VDOT

Atlantic Contracting & Materials Co., Inc.
Concrete pavement

Long Fence Co., Inc.
Fencing

Moore Brothers Co., Inc.
Electrical utilities

Payne's Parking Designs Inc.
Pavement markings

Tavares Concrete Co., Inc.
Miscellaneous concrete

Webster & Webster, Inc.
Guardrail

Shirley Construction Company, LLC
Prime contractor, site preparation, package 3, VDOT

A-Annandale Inc.
Pavement markings

APAC-VA
Asphalt paving

Dominion Caisson
Bridge pilings

DRM Associates
Bridge deck forms

C. C. Johnson Co.
Clearing and grubbing

Long Fence Co., Inc.
Fencing

Mastec North American
Roadway lighting

Midasco, Inc.
Project signs and structures

Penn Line Services
Guardrail and grass seeding

Potomac Rebar Inc.
Bridge reinforcing steel

Ridge Limited
Roadway underdrain

Safety Grooving
Bridge deck grooving

Tavares Concrete Co., Inc.
Miscellaneous. concrete

Ultra Services, Inc.
Environmental controls

Environmental Quality Resources, LLC
Prime contractor, site preparation, package 4, SI

Janis Rettaliata
Photography

Consolidated Engineering Services, Inc.
Integrated building services

CADDMicrosystems, Inc.
3-D computer modeling for artifact installations

Crystalizations Systems, Inc.
Mannequin and medium artifact exhibit cases

Design and Production, Inc.
Exhibit barrier system

Dorfmann Museum Figures, Inc.
Mannequins

Helmut Guenschel, Inc.
Large storefront exhibit cases

Washington Workplace
Furnishings

Metro Services
Furnishings installation

Summary Design an

Task Name	Start	Finish	1989				1990				1991				1992				199	
			Q1	Q2	Q3	Q4	Q1	Q2	Q3	Q4	Q1	Q2	Q3	Q4	Q1	Q2	Q3	Q4	Q1	Q2
Planning Activities	**Fri 9/1/89**	**Fri 5/31/96**																		
Site Selection Studies	Fri 9/1/89	Fri 11/30/90																		
Congressional Authority for Design	Mon 5/1/95	Mon 5/1/95																		
Master Planning	Mon 5/1/95	Fri 5/31/96																		
Design Activities	**Fri 10/11/96**	**Tue 6/1/99**																		
Programming & Schematic Design	Fri 10/11/96	Fri 5/23/97																		
Design Development	Fri 4/25/97	Thu 8/28/97																		
Construction Documents	Thu 8/28/97	Tue 6/1/99																		
Construction Activities	**Thu 6/1/00**	**Fri 12/5/03**																		
Site Preparation Package	Thu 6/1/00	Wed 8/1/01																		
Groundbreaking Ceremony	Wed 10/25/00	Wed 10/25/00																		
Facility Construction	Wed 4/11/01	Fri 12/5/03																		
Sitework Package	Tue 1/1/02	Fri 5/30/03																		
Interchange Construction	Mon 12/2/02	Fri 12/5/03																		
Wetlands Mitigation	Mon 4/7/03	Mon 11/3/03																		
Move-In Activities	**Mon 3/3/03**	**Mon 12/15/03**																		
Artifact Move-In	Mon 3/3/03	Fri 12/5/03																		
Opening Day	Mon 12/15/03	Mon 12/15/03																		

▬▬▬ Task   ▬▬▬ Progress   ◆ Milestone

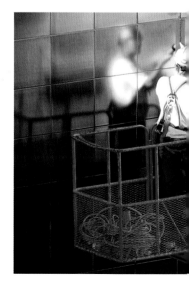

onstruction Schedule

	994		1995				1996				1997				1998				1999				2000				2001				2002				2003				2004			
	Q3	Q4	Q1	Q2	Q3	Q4	Q1	Q2	Q3	Q4	Q1	Q2	Q3	Q4	Q1	Q2	Q3	Q4	Q1	Q2	Q3	Q4	Q1	Q2	Q3	Q4	Q1	Q2	Q3	Q4	Q1	Q2	Q3	Q4	Q1	Q2	Q3	Q4	Q1	Q2	Q3	Q4

Design and Construction Lessons Learned

1. Purpose/vision/schedule. Most museum design and construction projects are long-term enterprises. A decade—or even two—can easily pass before a worthy concept is translated into construction documents and then into real bricks and mortar. During that decade or more, *be consistent about the need for and purpose of the project*. Key staff or board changes can bring significant changes to vision and schedule. While there may be excellent reasons for scaling back or redefining the project, when you do it midstream, you take the risk of leaving doubt among staff and external supporters. Significant changes should be announced with great care, with explanation, and after consultation with all the key stakeholders, including staff. Do not base your schedule on the best-case scenario; always think about what delays can mean to your opening events and your fundraising. You have no direct control over Government funding sources (or their timing), the economy, and the weather, but they can all drive your schedule off track or onto a new track.

2. Architect selection. When most of us think of selecting an architect, we think in terms of *design*. We're attracted to designs on paper or existing buildings that are similar in purpose, scale, and ambience to what we have in mind for our project. There are at least two other aspects of architect selection that are equally important. The first is the architect's *willingness to learn and willingness to teach*. Architects must learn the unique vocabulary of the museum world and come to truly understand your needs. And they have to teach you about a whole new world, and your vocabulary will expand, too. The second additional aspect for you to judge is the architect's ability to *manage* a large, complex project. If the firm can't account for the many subcontractors who will be called into the job, can't keep deadlines, and doesn't follow through on details, even the best concept design won't become a reality.

3. Technical liaison. Someone on the museum's direct payroll—even if it's a part-time employee—must be designated as project manager, with the *in-house technical expertise* to handle the contracting details, understand the legal issues related to a design and construction project, and speak the language of the industry and the museum. This may be in addition to someone else on the team who is managing the programmatic aspects of the project.

4. Programming. While this may be one of the most frustrating exercises of the first phase of design, it is probably the most important. Programming is the *formal exploration of your needs* as related to functional spaces and the proximity of those spaces. The architect should explain the process in advance, prepare you for the grueling repetitiveness of it, and ensure that the "programmer" understands your language and needs in advance. It is harder than it sounds to think through all the processes, activities, and interactions that will take place within a space that exists only in our minds, and usually no two minds envision that space exactly the same!

5. Functional needs vs. the "extras." In a well-balanced project, *all the projected purposes of the space are identified,* justified, and planned for in a manner that reflects the agreed-upon project goals. Even with that said, however, in an environment where dollars are limited—and that describes most museum projects—a competition can easily develop between proponents of "functional" spaces, like collections storage and exhibit areas, and those who identify needs that may be considered more peripheral to the project, like a nice conference room and special events spaces. Avoid the competition, or at least try, by including everyone in the programming exercise and then sharing and reviewing all the identified needs. It is a fact of museum life that most of our projects depend on external sources of funds, which bring with them their own new needs for space. The traditional museum staff member may call these requirements bells and whistles or window dressing, at best. But catering kitchens, storage spaces for banquet tables, holding areas for plants, and even liquor cabinets have found their way into most new museum designs. They are a part of doing business.

6. Fundraising. If you have brought professional development officers and researchers in to support your project, *make them a part of your museum team*. If the capital campaign team is to be successful, they have to understand and believe in your project just as passionately as you do—or at least it has to appear that way. Make them believers. Get them involved in what you do programmatically. And equally important, be prepared to *learn from them*. The development world has its own language, its own way of doing business. You will probably be working with development professionals during your entire museum career, so museum staff—not just managers—should make the effort to learn the language and tools of the trade. Share fundraising goals and strategy with staff and other insiders; celebrate the successes together.

7. Information flow. Because we are usually juggling business as usual *and* the management of a new design project, it is difficult to keep everyone informed on the details and the decisions. *The director, project manager, and program manager must take responsibility for keeping everyone informed—and for listening.* This advice cannot be overstated. Information must flow down from the director and up from the working troops to ensure an efficient project. If the organization is having communications problems before it takes on a major new project, those problems will grow exponentially. And for goodness sake, don't let your director get surprised by any of the details!

8. Environmental assessment. The environmental assessment is actually part of the architect's design work, along with things like geotechnical reports, risk analyses, traffic studies, and view shed sketches, to name just a few parts of the work. The EA will be time-consuming and expensive; the schedule for the work cannot be predicted with total accuracy; it will require many experts as subcontractors; it will be of great interest to the public; the findings could prompt you to rethink your entire concept; it could even bring a complete halt to your work. *Take an active role in the environmental assessment and don't underestimate its potential impact on your project.*

9. Design reviews. Architectural designs proceed formally from concept design, to design development, to schematic design (approximately at the 35 percent completion stage), to construction documentation that is 65 percent, then 95 percent, and finally 100 percent complete. At each milestone, the architect presents growing mountains of blueprints, artist concepts, 3-D views, technical specifications, and ever more precise cost estimates. *Staff review at every phase of the design is the most important thing the museum can provide!* It is grueling work; it demands attention to detail; museum staff must learn how to read blueprints; it seemingly never ends. If you are to go on to construction with confidence in your design, you must know the design as well as the architect. Change orders during construction—or, even worse, redoing work after you start occupying the space—is expensive, disruptive, and disappointing. Every outlet and data port location, every material selection, every furniture selection, every hangar door mechanism, every plumbing fixture must be reviewed by the staff who will use and maintain them. Design review is an enormous job; staff will need the time and perhaps the training to accomplish this new duty.

10. Contingency planning. Don't wait until your best laid plans are dashed—or your boss or board question your final design and its cost estimate—to formally plan contingencies. Contingencies could include phasing the project, scaling it down, or postponing construction. *Work with your architect to translate the contingencies into documentation* that reflects these alternatives and provides cost estimates for the different scenarios. Using this strategy, at any point during the design phase, the drawings and specs will reflect your complete build-out but also give you backup room if you need it without paying the architect to rethink and redraw all the construction documents.

11. Visualizations. *Nothing helps bring a design to life as well as computer-generated visualizations* of your design, populated by artifacts, exhibits, and people. These "virtual tours" are based on the actual computer-aided design drawings produced by the architect and modeled further by experts in that field. It is worth the cost; it is expensive; but it may be one of your best selling tools. According to Interface MultiMedia's Jeff Pullford, who produced NASM's renderings and animation, there is a wide range of costs for this kind of work. The ranges shown below (in 2004 $US) assume that you already have your 3-D computer-aided design architectural drawings in hand:

Interior environments: To model (add color, texture, lighting, reflections, shadows, people, objects, etc.) a typical interior environment, like a gallery, room, or lobby (all four sides), the costs are in the range of $1,800–4,400.

Exterior environment: To model a street scene, cityscape, or the outside of a building, the range is $3,800–10,300.

Animation: To animate the models, the costs are an additional $1,800–4,300 per minute, depending on complexity, special effects, etc.

12. Visitor studies. It's important to know who your visitors will be, what expectations they bring to the destination, where they will come from, how they will get there, how long they are likely to stay, what conveniences they will need during their visit. This data will help you plan your broad program objectives, assist you with transportation planning, convince donors that you will have an impact (and that their sponsorship will be noticed), justify revenue-generation strategies, and serve as ammunition when you approach local governments for support. Visitors equal economic impact. Don't forget that. Plan to capture as much of that impact for yourself as you can. *You should start your visitor studies early*; they are required as part of the formal environmental assessment, but don't wait until then. If you have a visitor base already and are planning an extension, interview your visitors. Contract with an expert in the field of visitor forecasting. *Work with economic forecasters to translate that data into economic projections*. And if the planning or fundraising for your project takes decades, you must revisit your forecasts to verify your data. Populations, residential development, public transportation infrastructure, or a booming/waning economy can all drive your forecasts up or down, and you need to take the pulse more than once.

13. Revenue generation. We tend to think along traditional lines when it comes to including revenue-generating pieces to our museum projects: food service, gift shops, theaters. What else can we add? Simulators (or the latest technology that gives visitors the physical experience we're looking to impart), high-tech imaging opportunities, personalized services, catering, special events, highly customized tour packages, special experiences with the collections, concerts, lectures, instruction. What physical infrastructure requirements are demanded by the venues you select? *With your architect, ensure that your design can accommodate the revenue-generating ideas you want to pursue* (doors have to be large enough and floors sturdy enough to accommodate simulators, for example). But don't get bogged down in the details if your design is 10 years ahead of actual construction (you can figure out where the ketchup dispensers will go later or what kind of french fry unit to spec); there is a lot of change in the business-end of things. You need to stay as flexible as possible as long as possible, but think through the major physical demands in advance: door size, floor loading, data needs, utility requirements, etc.

14. Know your neighbors. Just about every region has marketing and economic development staff these days, and there are many regional visitor attraction consortia. Pool talent and resources. Don't be a competitor with the zoo and the dance company; *be a complementary piece of the bigger cultural scene*. Share information; plan and strategize together. Staff or volunteers from a regional visitors' center may be available to work at your site with you!

15. Site work-building construction coordination. NASM was blessed with a significant contribution from the Commonwealth of Virginia. The state provided all the site infrastructure required—from clearing the site, bringing in utilities, paving the parking lot, and providing a new intersection off Route 28. However, the work was provided under the direction of the Virginia Department of Transportation, who contracted for the work. The building construction contract was managed by the Smithsonian. Coordinating the issues between the two communities of contractors and contract managers required constant vigilance, as the *site work had a most direct impact on the building*—placement of utility manholes, loading dock elevations, backfilling, sidewalk paving, fire hydrants, drainage. Central management—rather than dual—of the design and construction of both site work and building construction is highly recommended. If a donor steps up to the plate and offers the site work, try to secure the cash and let and manage your own contracts; if they elect to stay your on-site partner, be prepared to expend extra resources—and patience—in coordinating the effort.

16. Partnering. Partnering is a popular word in the construction industry, and it means about what you would expect: *sharing the vision and commitment for a job well done as a team*. It's relatively easy to meet for a day or two and document the importance of partnering and the areas of greatest mutual concern—safety, schedule, profit, and budget—but it's much harder to keep the ideals in mind when you find yourself in the midst of problem-solving. In a large, complex project, there are going to be disputes between the architect and the general contractor, the owner and the architect, the code officials and everyone. It must be impossible to catch every detail during the design phase, but you will catch them during construction or inspections. That's the truest test of partnering: remember that this project belongs to the team, and if one part of the team falters, the entire team takes the fall. Partnering requires meeting together as a group several times during the course of the project; plan sessions as you gear up for major milestones or if you have a specific problem to address, and don't forget to have a partnering session as you approach close-out and punchlist. If the staff who are going to occupy the building and staff it have not been intimately involved during design and construction, this last partnering session would be an ideal time to fold them into the process. They may think they will be moving into a completed building with all systems working; that may not be the case, and now is the time to get them used to the idea and make them part of the process of closing out the construction phase.

17. No rest for the owner. Just because you've lived with the planning and design effort for years, don't think the owner can now sit back and enjoy watching the construction show and not be involved every day! Even with the best construction drawings in the world, the owner needs to stay enthusiastically involved in the construction process. Material samples that may have passed muster five years ago, may no longer be available; you need to approve the substitute. The museum's new manager of revenue generation has a great scheme for running an outdoor café, which is going to require a major reworking of the civil drawings, new utility requirements, new sidewalks; can you do it without impacting your opening day? The ABC Company just introduced a better trash storage system; can you make the substitute within the space designed at the loading dock? Shop drawings bring to light a roof decking hanger that is unsightly; what's acceptable? And the list goes on. *Assign a single point of contact to work with the construction team*, who is empowered to bring resolution to these types of issues. Your representative should be intimately familiar with the design and know whom to go to on the museum's staff to get feedback.

18. Commissioning. There are many definitions of this term. *Define what you want in the arena of building systems tests, verifications, efficiency measurements, and related activities during the design phase*. Decide what tasks you want your general contractor to perform as part of building construction and what, if any, third-party assignments—at an extra cost—are important. And remember that all building systems interact! Bring your building maintenance engineer into the process during design if you can; if not, bring him/her on board no later than when the major building systems are being installed.

19. Value engineering. If you tell your building contractor to review the design and determine if your new museum can be built "better, faster, cheaper" than your architect told you it could, be prepared to evaluate those ideas quickly. And don't be surprised if your architect, who has lived with your project for years, doesn't immediately embrace all these new ideas from a GC who has been on the project for eight weeks. *Review the cost-savings ideas from every angle*: does the finished project still meet your programmatic needs; is the appearance acceptable; will the change lead to different maintenance expectations and costs in the future; is it the most efficient alternative and, if not, is it worth the savings; are there design costs associated with the change. If you're still in the midst of raising money to build your museum, you will welcome a decrease in construction costs, but keep remembering why you're building this structure and don't jeopardize your core objectives.

20. Safety. Unsafe activity on the job carries a cost you do not want to shoulder. Therefore, it is the highest priority for the entire team. It may sound like a worn-out phrase, but *safety is everyone's business*. And one individual must be assigned safety officer. However, everyone on the job should be comfortable with shutting down an activity he/she believes is unsafe. No one should expect access and safety requirements to be loosened for special visitors. You will select your general contractor, in part, based on the company's past safety record and the specific safety plan they submit as part of their proposal. But the best safety plan in the world is only as good as the people making decisions every day about how they will perform a particular task. Make safety a part of the job every day.

21. Utilities. In this era of deregulated utilities—most specifically, electrical providers—be aware of your choices during the design phase and *select your provider as you commence construction or before, if possible*. If your property can be served by multiple providers and if there is a conflict among them, it may have to be resolved by a state commission (or some other regional authority), which can take time you don't have. The lead time for ordering transformers can be long; you will need to have determined your provider so that their schedule for setting the transformers meshes with your general contractor's master construction schedule.

22. Construction contingency funds. New construction projects carry a construction contingency budget of 6–12 percent of the bid price to cover whatever "unknowns" you will encounter during construction (renovation projects carry an 8–15 percent contingency line item). There are the predictable unknowns, such as soil conditions that don't live up to the geotechnical surveys or blizzards that take away two weeks of work time. But there is another category that will eat up more of that budget: *design deficiencies*. Even the most competent architects are going to have coordination lapses in a complex project: discrepancies between the written specifications and the drawings, missing dimensions, disconnects between site drawings and building drawings, automated security needs that can't be supported by the electrical design. And if the owner was forced to repackage the drawings or scale them back or phase the project, the opportunities for such errors are multiplied significantly. *Design deficiencies are not necessarily a sign of a poor job by the architect; more likely it is a sign of the complexity of the job and the owner's changing needs.* For a large, complex project, design deficiencies average at 5 percent of the construction costs (we ran at less than 3 percent, a great track record). The best way to avoid such problems is careful review by the owner of the evolving design drawings, as discussed above (#9), but even then, you will miss something. You should work closely with the architect during this phase, who will be on-site with a "construction administration" team to resolve issues quickly with the general contractor. You may be able to make a case for the architect taking on financial responsibility for a change if the error is especially egregious (think about that when you review your contract with the architect). And you will want to track the reasons behind all your change orders: owner-initiated/program driven; design deficiencies; unknown conditions; related to phasing or cutting back the design; related to revenue-generating requirements.

23. Construction management. Most owners buy construction management services even before the construction contract has been let. CM personnel can help you evaluate the proposals and compare technical and procedural differences among the bidders. A well written justification of your choice can be worth its weight in gold if there is a protest by an unsuccessful bidder. And after construction starts, the CM can serve as your expert (or supplemental experts) in the field: to *review* shop drawings and submittals, to *inspect* work as it is done to ensure that the terms of the specifications are being met, to *negotiate* change orders, verifying that the contractor's estimates for changes and credits are fair and reasonable, and to *manage your close-out and punchlist*, which can number in the thousands of items. The owner should stay involved, however, in any negotiation sessions; while it's great to have a construction management team that is watching the dollars as well as the quality of workmanship, you may need to bring balance or compromise to the table from time to time during negotiations.

24. Room numbers. Granted, this sounds minor, but insist that your architect devises a room numbering system during the design phase that does not have to be reworked when it is time to assign room numbers on door signage. Your as-built drawings and your building automated system will be keyed to the architect's original designations; renumbering would be a headache you can avoid!!

25. Photographic documentation. If your project lends itself to remote time-lapse photography or a webcam, plan early. Pick your locations and understand the limitations and needs of your equipment (like electric). Be realistic about the budget that will be required for a dedicated server for a webcam or getting temporary electrical service to a remote pole or protecting a high-dollar 35mm camera from the elements. If you wait until construction starts or if you try to rely wholly on the generosity of in-kind donors, you may miss your opportunity. Most construction contracts call for regular professional photographic documentation of the ongoing construction. Consider adding monthly aerial photographs to that list and the services of a videographer to capture high-quality film of milestone activities. With the popularity of digital cameras, you may find yourself with an embarrassment of

riches. Everyone with a camera will take shots and send you their images. *Image management* can become a challenge. Think ahead to a filing system that is easy to add pictures to, and you'll need plenty of storage capacity. And caption the photos (most systems capture the date automatically). The work will be worth it: to document your project and to keep donors and prospective donors enthused about your progress. Share the photos and movies on your web site, on bulletin boards, and in newsletters.

26. Counting and screening visitors. One of the most frequent questions you will get after opening is how many visitors came today. There are several high-tech counting systems on the market, and you should be looking at the options during design, because they will require power and data. Screening your visitors to meet security requirements is another need that should be defined as early as possible, and think ahead to the most stringent requirements that you can imagine. *Plan the building for the worst-case scenario*, so you will have room enough for magnetometers, search tables, and personnel should you need them some day, as well as the power and data needed to support them. Your code officials will tell you how much width you need at entrances for safely evacuating your visitors; that calculation needs to take into account any equipment or furniture associated with the security operation that could impede an evacuation.

27. Proprietary designs. There are *pre-engineering building systems on the market that may meet your basic needs*. These could save you money and time, even if they must be customized, with your architect, to meet your program's needs. "Brick and mortar" is not the only way to build. Insist that your architect explore such options. Within your design, you may also have pieces of the project that are not under direct control, like a theater or food court, for example. A vendor, like IMAX®, for example, will have very specific design requirements for a theater that will not be shared with the architect until you have a signed contract in your hands. While the architect can make informed decisions, based on comparable theaters, he/she will not have the final specs until the IMAX® contract is in hand. Factor that into your schedule. Time your negotiations so that your architect doesn't have to guess. Reworking is costly and takes a bite out of your schedule. The same can apply to the kitchens of a food vendor, who may require a specifically sized grease trap, which is one of the first things that the general contractor will need to build into the floor and foundation; if you wait until the last hours to select a food vendor, you could be doing some de-construction.

28. Transportation studies. Obviously, visitors have to be able to drive to or get public transportation to (or walk to) your location. If you are in a region that is already facing transportation challenges (crowded roads, failing interchanges, costly public transportation upgrades, construction), you may add to the problem. At the earliest possible moment (and as part of your environmental assessment), join forces with the transportation planners of the region. Learn transportation-speak; identify the major issues and players; join a regional transportation association if there is one; keep the government transportation officials updated on your plans. There may be state-wide transportation enhancement grant money available for regional signage; there may be Federal money available for transportation studies (keep your local members of Congress apprised of any issues that their constituents may raise). Don't assume that street signs and interchange signs are

free; you will probably have to reimburse the county or state for them. Work with local tourism officials and the transportation experts to determine where and how to place signage so that it best directs traffic. *Update transportation studies* if more than five years have passed since your last one.

29. Furniture. During your design work, you will help the architect identify what furnishings are required for your space, to include office furniture, workstations, public seating, trash containers, work benches, etc. If you expect to go to bid on the construction of your job immediately, then you can direct your architect to select the exact furniture you will need, to include models, options, colors, and fabrics. However, *if years might go by between the conclusion of your design and the start of your construction, hold off on the specifics*. Identify what you will be needing and where it will go; ensure that power and data are located in the right places to support your furniture plan; but do not spend days looking at different chairs, desks, and work stations. Ask your architect to give you two or three price options based on the quality of the pieces, but stop there. There is too much change in the world of furnishings to lock into product selection early in the process: pieces become obsolete; companies go out of business; chairs improve; patents expire; fabrics become discontinued; and your new director may hate what the previous director selected. Give yourself several months before going to bid to finish your work. You can include the furniture package as part of the general contractor's work, and this is highly recommended for workstations that are hard-wired and otherwise integrated into the building systems and structure. You may want to procure your own mobile pieces and save the overhead, but know that you will be expending considerable staff time in managing the process.

30. Interior signage. It is almost impossible to figure out in advance all your signage needs, but your architect will help you with your basic package (or try to provide it all if that's your desire). I recommend that your architect *design a family of signage* and recommend placement, especially for way-finding signage and any signs that will require extra blocking or support, but you need to stay flexible as long as possible when it comes to the actual wording, directions for arrows, size of type, and the like. This is especially true with a very large building that is uniquely designed, or if your program is continuing to change up to opening day and beyond, or if your donor recognition program is still subject to change (if Mr. Big Bucks comes along the week before opening, it would be to your advantage to be able to provide signage for the Bucks Gallery pronto). Your general contractor will have a subcontractor for graphics and signage; you may want to establish a relationship with that sub for post-opening changes and additions.

31. Accessibility issues. Standards for physical accessibility, and your goals as an organization to provide *universal accessibility for all visitors, will evolve over time*. Again, if there is a time gap between the completion of design and start of construction, have your architect research any changes in the law or your governing organization's expectations. If the design no longer meets code or expectations, make the changes before construction starts.

32. Construction team changes. You will get a list of key participants from your general contractor before work starts, along with their qualifications to manage and execute your project. The same applies to the subs. During the course of a long project, you can expect some changes in staffing; your GC must provide notice of the changes and must provide you with equally qualified personnel. But some people will leave your site mid-stream; they may quit the company, get promotions to other jobs; they may not be the right personality for your job after all. As the owner, you should not hesitate to express opinions about these changes, and be especially aware as the job closes out. You may discover that the senior folks who were so effective in bringing your project through most of the challenges of the job will move on to other high-profile projects, leaving Team B in their place. Team B will probably be equally qualified, but you will not know them as well, and there can be communications problems as a result during the critical close-out/punchlist period. And Team B may not have the same powers of persuasion with the subs. A *partnering session* before close-out will give everyone an opportunity to assess the changes and recommit to a successful end of the project.

33. Weather delays. If it can flood, storm, snow, or blow, it will do so during the construction of your project. Your general contractor's schedule will include float to account for weather delays typical in your region. But if at all possible, *do not select an exact opening date at the outset of construction*, so that unusual weather delays (or other problems) can be addressed without working all the crews 24/7. Your contractor will also give you his/her assessment of weather impacts on a monthly basis if it's in your contract; have your construction manager review the impact statement to determine if you are in agreement with it. It may have rained 20 days out of 31 last month, but if you were working inside the building on finishes, it might not have impacted your job.

34. Accommodating beneficial occupancy and special tours. If you have a fixed opening date, you will probably require early occupancy so that you can start bringing in your artifacts, building your displays, and installing your servers. *Co-occupancy of the space by contractors and owners requires a tremendous amount of trust by both parties*. If you can avoid it, you should. If you can't, you need a carefully written plan and agreement: who can use what equipment; who can access what parts of the building; when can doors be open; who has responsibility for security of what; if something comes up missing, how do you investigate the loss; whose insurance is responsible for what; what can you ask and not ask the contractor to do for you; and the list just keeps going. You will need a full-time on-site owner manager to make it work. And if you are still fundraising, and who isn't, you will want to bring VIPs and potential donors to the site. Beyond the safety issues discussed earlier, you may need to be concerned with unsightly construction trash, equipment in the way of what you want to showcase, wet paint, stairs without handrails in place yet, elevators being tested (that may stop in between floors), wet concrete, cold or hot rooms, dirt and debris, and this list goes on even further. But you will want to carefully coordinate those visits as well as the visits of members of the media, the hospitality industry, government officials, etc. You always need to scout your route of travel through your building in advance and have an alternative plan in mind in the event that a door that was unlocked at 10:00 is not accessible at noon; that lights that were working that morning are not working that afternoon because they are testing the generator. Make the visit an "exploration experience"; make sure your special visitors are kept safe; be ready with explanations of what they are seeing and why it is in the condition it is. Always picture in

advance what photographs or descriptions might come from these sneak previews.

35. Statistics. People want to know *facts and figures*: how many tons of steel, gallons of paint, miles of duct, dimensions of spaces, and so on. Include these fun facts on your web site and handouts. Involve the contractor in coming up with them.

36. Use of CADD for artifact placement planning. NASM's collections and exhibit team made *extensive use of models and automated tools* to determine the precise locations of the artifacts in the hangars. This saved trial-and-error reckoning and the time associated with moving big objects several times. The automated system even helped us order the rigging cables precut, which saved time and money.

37. Mechanical systems. A museum pays extra attention to the environment it provides for the safekeeping of its artifacts and comfort of its visitors. Our planning started with *defining the parameters required for the long-term display and storage of the collection*. The architect's mechanical-electrical-plumbing (MEP) experts had to understand the nature of the collection (and that's the owner's responsibility). And even beyond a specific and stable temperature and humidity level, you must consider airflow that might interfere with a glider or fragile hanging satellite, and those diffusers won't be aimed until the last minute, so you need to keep access cleared. And the MEP system of any modern, complex building interfaces with the building's security systems and the building automated system (BAS). And it takes months to balance and fully integrate all this complex equipment! It's a costly part of the building, but if you want your objects to last forever—and that's our business—you can't cut corners here.

38. Prototyping. NASM started planning its displays of the collection many years before move-in began in 2003. The exhibit cases were specified after much research and after we had visited several museums and factories. We ordered prototypes of the three sizes and types of cases, loaded them with a variety of artifacts, and made changes before going into production. In fact, we prototyped an entire display area at the Museum on the Mall before we went to production on the system. *Using these prototypes, we pre-loaded each case*, carefully noted the display requirements for each, and photographed the placements. This sped up the actual installations considerably, because there were few surprises in the field.

39. Archiving. Save your *project documentation as an archived record set*. This includes blueprints and specifications, change order records, photo documentation, correspondence, contracting documents, site selection justifications, approvals, and budget data, just to name a few important categories.

40. Recognizing the team. It takes a legion of people and organizations to build or renovate a museum. Everyone brings their special talents and skills to the big job, and *the entire team needs to be valued and recognized*. Unfortunately, with the pressures of opening day and raising funds, it is easy to overlook important members of the team. We recommend a tiered approach to recognizing the achievements of such a large group, from the black tie galas to thank the major donors to awards ceremonies to reward key personnel, to ceremonies that include the entire workforce. Work hard to be inclusive; plan some activity that will touch every hand that helped build your project.

41. Selecting a general contractor. You will be looking at the prospective general contractors' *technical prowess and their best price*. You should receive distinct proposals for each. If you do not have the technical expertise to evaluate the proposals, seek help from an objective construction manager; that same expert may also play a useful role for you in the field after construction starts. Look for a proposal that addresses all the legal requirements of your request for proposal, but also clearly tells you how your project will be built. Look at the credentials of the key players who will be on your team and beware of substitutions. Check safety records on other jobs, as well as the rate of change orders realized on other jobs. Has this GC built buildings like the one you have designed? Will this GC be sensitive to the special needs of a museum, the public, and artifacts? If you are still actively fundraising, talk to the GC about job site access for fundraising purposes and for media opportunities. During presentations, observe how staged or unstaged the performances are. Does each team member have a very narrow role to play, or does everyone know the entire game plan? If you are the lone museum professional on the selection team, ask lots of questions and pay attention not only to the answers but the spirit in which the replies are given. As it was with the architect, you and the GC will be teaching one another during this project. Can you learn from this GC; do you think you can teach the GC team about your unique world?

42. Design-build. There are *two possible routes to designing and building* your project. You can independently design and then independently construct your building; you competitively select the architect, and then, with design in hand, you select a general contractor. This is the route we followed with the Udvar-Hazy project. We discovered during construction that tension can build between architect and general contractor, but this is to be expected and serves as a system of checks and balances. The architect wants to ensure that the GC delivers what the architect designed. Alternatively, you can select a single team that will provide both services, with one party—either the GC or the architect—taking the lead. The latter is called design-build. Greater cooperation could be expected if both parties are contractually on the same team. As the owner, you have a single point of contact to resolve conflicts, and you do not play the role of arbiter between the two. But you may sacrifice some amount of control over the project. Some architects do not participate in design-build partnerships, so you may find yourself limited in your selection of creative architects. If your project is a long-term one (it may actually be years before you can expect to have money enough in hand to build), you may not find a GC willing to enter the relationship. There are pros and cons to both approaches; explore them.

43. Legal advice. A building project is complex, expensive, and exciting, but it's also an opportunity for conflict. And even with the best of partnering intentions, you should seek legal counsel and review before signing any contracts or modifications to those contracts. Your agreements with all contractors should clearly spell out a game plan for any deficiencies, unforeseen conditions, failures, accidents, savings, or other unanticipated events. Get the best legal advice you can, draft a contract that provides protection that is as complete as possible, and then have a professional negotiate for you. And most importantly, know that all parties must adhere to the terms, conditions, and specifications of that contract.

Aircraft and Spacecraft Installed for Opening Day   by Bill Doole

The National Air and Space Museum started moving artifacts to the Steven F. Udvar-Hazy Center in March 2003 in anticipation of the December 2003 opening. The relocation will continue over the next several years. The Center was sized to accommodate some 200 aircraft, 135 space vehicles, and thousands of small objects. The following list does not include small artifacts in exhibit cases or aircraft engines.

Aircraft

A

Aichi M6A1 Seiran (Clear Sky Storm)
Arado Ar 234B-2 Blitz (Lightning)
Arrow Sport A2-60

B

Bede BD-5A/B
Bell UH-1H Iroquois
Bell XV-15 Tiltrotor
Benoist-Korn
Boeing 307 Stratoliner
Boeing 367-80
Boeing B-29-35-MO Superfortress
    Enola Gay
Boeing FB-5 Hawk
Boeing P-26A Peashooter
Boeing-Stearman N2S-5 Kaydet
Bowlus BA-100 Baby Albatross
Bowlus-Du Pont Albatross *Falcon*
Bücker Bü-133C Jungmeister
    (Young Master)

C

Caudron G.4
Concorde
Curtiss F6C-4 *Gulfhawk 1A*
Curtiss P-40E Warhawk

D

Dassault Cargo Fanjet Falcon 20C
De Havilland-Canada D.H.C.1 Chipmunk
Delta Wing Mariah M-9
Delta Wing Model 162
Delta Wing Phoenix 6
Delta Wing Phoenix 6B
Delta Wing Phoenix Streak
Delta Wing Phoenix Viper 175

E

Eipper-Formance Cumulus 10

F

Focke-Achgelis Fa 330A
Focke-Wulf Fw 190F-8/R1
Frankfort TG-1A (Cinema)

G

Gates Learjet 23
Grob 102 Standard Astir III
Grumman A-6E Intruder
Grumman F6F-3 Hellcat
Grumman F8F-2 Bearcat

Grumman G-21 Goose
Grumman G-22 *Gulfhawk II*
Grunau Baby II B-2

H

Hawker Hurricane Mk.IIC

J

Junkers Ju 52/3m (CASA 352L)

K

Kawanishi N1K2-Ja Shiden Kai (George)
Kawasaki Ki-45 Toryu NICK
Kreider-Reisner KR-34C
Kugisho Ohka 22 (Cherry Blossom)

L

Langley Aerodrome A
Lockheed 5C Vega *Winnie Mae*
Lockheed P-38J-10-LO Lightning
Lockheed SR-71 Blackbird
Lockheed X-35 Joint Strike Fighter
Loudenslager Laser 200

M

MacCready Gossamer Albatross
Manta Pterodactyl Fledgling
McDonnell F-4S-44 Phantom II
Mignet-Crosley HM.14 Pou du Ciel
Mikoyan-Gurevich MiG-15bis FAGOT
Mikoyan-Gurevich MiG-21F-13 FISHBED-C
Monnett Moni
Monocoupe 110 Special *Little Butch*

N

Nagler-Rolz NR 54 V2
NAF N3N-3 *Yellow Peril*
Nieuport 28
North American F-86A Sabre
North American P-51C
    Mustang *Excalibur III*
Northrop N-1M

P

Piper J-3 Cub
Piper PA-18 Super Cub
Pitts Special S-1C *Little Stinker*

R

Republic P-47D-30-RA Thunderbolt
Rockwell Shrike Commander 500S
Rutan VariEze

S

Schweizer SGU 2-22 EK
Sharp DR 90 *Nemesis*

SPAD XVI
Sportwings Valkyrie
Stinson L-5 Sentinel
Sukoi Su-26M

T

Travel Air D4D *Pepsi Skywriter*

V

Vought F4U-1D Corsair
Vought-Sikorsky OS2U-3 Kingfisher

W

Weedhopper JC-24C

Space Artifacts

A

AGM-86A Cruise Missile
Airborne Infrared Telescope
AMRAAM Missile
Antisatellite Missile
Apollo Command Module boilerplate
Apollo Service Module Propulsion System
Ariane 4 rocket model
Atlas-Agena launch console
Atlas-Centaur rocket model
Atoll Missile

B

Bell No. 2 rocket belt

C

CDC 3800 computer

D

Delta 3914 model

E

Echo 1 communications satellite

F

Falcon AGM-76A
Ftitz X guided bomb

G

Gemini VII
Goddard 1935 A-Series Rocket

H

H-1 rocket engine
H-I rocket model
H-II rocket model
Hs 117 Schmetterling Missile

Hs 293 A-1 Missile
Hs 298 V2 Missile
HVAR Missile

I

IUE control and display system

J

Jupiter S-3 rocket engine

M

Massively Parallel Processor
    Expansion and Processor Units
Matador TM-61C Cruise Missile
Mercury capsule *Big Joe*
Mercury capsule 15B *Freedom 7 II*
MIDAS Series III infrared sensor
Mighty Mouse Missile
Mobile Quarantine Facility
Mother Ship Model

N

Navaho missile and booster model
Navaho rocket engine

R

Redstone rocket engine
Regulus 1 Cruise Missile
Relay 1 communications satellite
Rheintochter Missile
Ritchey Mirror grinding machine
Ruhrstahl X-4 Missile

S

Space Shuttle *Enterprise*
Spacelab Instrument Pointing System
Spacelab Laboratory Module
Spacelab Subsystems Igloo
Spacelab Transfer Tunnel, Joggle Section
Sparrow 2 Missile
Styx Missile

T

Talos Missile
Tiny Tim Missile
Titan I rocket engine
Titan IIIC rocket model
Titan IIIE Centaur rocket model

V

Vega Solar System Probe Bus and
    Landing Apparatus

Z

Zuni Missile

Exhibitions Team and Lighting Design Components

by Frank Florentine

Building Lighting Designers

Fisher Marantz Stone, New York, Paul Marantz and Scott Hershman

Exhibitions

Exhibit Designer:
William Jacobs, National Air and Space Museum (NASM)

Case Artifact Design:
Linda King, NASM

Graphics Designers:
Beatrice Mowry, Barbara Brennan, Jennifer Carlton, NASM

Lighting Designer:
Frank A. Florentine, FIES, LC, NASM

Special Events Lighting Designer:
David Adcock, NASM

Lighting Equipment

1. Reflected ceiling lights:
Aviation hangar light shelf
Type: Surface-mounted metal halide uplight with 5H2V NEMA distribution pattern, lockable swivel knuckle, custom louver
Job identifier: Type FF
Color temperature: 3,700K
Wattage: 1,000 each; Voltage: 277
Quantity: 95 per side, 190 total
Manufacturer: Cooper Lighting, Inc.

2. Light track:
Throughout building and exhibit barrier
Type: Surface-mounted single- and double-circuit extruded aluminum track
Job identifier: Type FZ-2, FZ-3, FZ-4
Ampacity: 20 amp bus bar; Voltage: 120
Manufacturer: Lighting Services Inc.

3. Light track fixtures:
Throughout building and exhibit barrier
Type: Track-mounted metal halide adjustable accent light with integral ballast, UV filter, spread lens and hood
Job identifier: Type FC, FG, UH1, UH2
Color temperature: 3,000K
Wattage: All PAR 30: FC=70; FG=100; UH1 & UH2=39; Voltage: 120
Quantity: FC=550; FG=238; UH1 & UH2=55
Manufacturer: Lighting Services Inc.

4. Light towers:
Aviation hangar and space hangar
Type: Portable light tower with concealed power, data lines, maximum height 9 meters +/-, six 20 amp, 120 volt circuits, maximum footprint 1.5 meters, with mounting rings for 12 lights; multi-cable connectors, utility outlets at base; secured controls
Quantity: 10
Manufacturer: Mr. Dave Paine, RibbonLift, Inc.
 1065 24th Avenue SW
 Owatonna, MN 55060
 (507) 451-9604; FAX: (507) 451-2688
 riblift@mnic.net

5. Light tower light fixtures
Type: Pipe-mounted ceramic metal halide adjustable spot/floodlight with polished aluminum reflector, cast aluminum housing, externally operated rotating lens ring, integral ballast, safety cable, combination snoot color frame holder, pipe clamp, power cable with parallel blade connector
Quantity: 12 per light tower
Job identifier: Type FBJ; ETC Source Four HID PAR
Color temperature: 3,000K
Wattage: 150; Voltage: 120
Manufacturer: ETC

6. Special light fixtures:
5-degree ellipsoidal light fixture
Type: Pipe-mounted ceramic metal halide adjustable spot/floodlight with faceted borosilicate reflector with multi-layer dichroic coating, cast aluminum housing, rotating shutter assembly, 20 gauge stainless-steel shutters in tri-plane assembly, integral ballast, safety cable, combination snoot color frame holder, pipe clamp, power cable with parallel blade connector, plastic Fresnel lens
Quantity: Two available for testing for lighting SR 71
Job identifier: NA; ETC Source Four HID 5°
Color temperature: 3,000K
Wattage: 150; Voltage: 120
Manufacturer: ETC

7. Mannequin exhibit cases
Quantity: 10
Lighting: Fiber optic lighting, all glass fibers, 24 points per case
Illuminator: Low voltage, MR16, 100W Schott H-2
Case manufacturer: Crystalizations Systems, Inc.
 640 Broadway Avenue
 Holbrook, NY 11741
 (631) 567-0888; FAX: (631) 567-4007
 Patricia Ellenwood, President; Dan Murray
 CSIstorage@aol.com
 http://www.CSIstorage.com

8. Medium exhibit cases
Quantity: 22
Lighting: Fluorescent tubes with UV filter, off/on switches, motion sensor
Case manufacturer: Crystalizations Systems, Inc.
 640 Broadway Avenue
 Holbrook, NY 11741
 (631) 567-0888; FAX: (631) 567-4007
 Patricia Ellenwood, President; Dan Murray
 CSIstorage@aol.com
 http://www.CSIstorage.com

9. Large storefront exhibit cases
Quantity: 10
Lighting: Fluorescent tubes with UV filter, off/on switches, motion sensor
Manufacturer: Helmut Guenschel, Inc.
 10 Emala Avenue
 Baltimore, MD 21220
 (410) 686-5900; FAX: (410) 687-9342
 Attn: Cynthia Shaffer, General Manager
 cynthias@guenschel.com
 www.guenschel.com

10. Exhibit barrier system
Quantity: approximately 900 linear meters
Manufacturer: Design and Production, Inc.
 7110 Rainwater Place
 Lorton, VA 22079-1521
 (703) 550-8640; FAX: (703) 339-0926
 Attn: Debbie Cone
 dcone@d-and-p.com

11. Transparency boxes
Type: Ultra-low profile transparency box; image size 1,475 x 915 mm, with day-night transparency
Quantity: 5
Lamp: T5 F80W/865 High Output Med. Bi-pin base
Color temperature: 6,500K
Wattage: 150; Voltage: 120
Manufacturer/supplier: Ihor Makara
 Infinite Photo & Imaging
 6707 Electronic Drive
 Springfield, VA 22151
 (703) 642-7077; FAX: (703) 354-5840
 ihor@infinit

Source Notes

Chapter 1

1 Letter, H. H. Arnold, Hq., Army Air Forces, to R. H. Fleet, President, Institute of the Aeronautical Sciences, 9 November 1945.

2 Smithsonian Institution (SI), "Report on the National Air Museum for the Year Ended June 30, 1949," *Smithsonian Report for 1949* (Washington, D.C.: U.S. Government Printing Office, 1950), 114–117. See also, Federal Works Agency, Public Buildings Administration, "Proposed National Air Museum, SI, Washington, D.C.," project 49.128, 24 June 1949.

3 Preston R. Bassett, Frederick C. Durant, William Littlewood, and Addison Rothrock, "Proposed Objectives and Plans for the National Air and Space Museum," report to Director S. Paul Johnson, 15 January 1965, 33–34.

4 Letter, Louis S. Casey to Neil November, 26 October 1966.

5 Letter, November to S. Paul Johnston, 10 April 1967.

6 Letter, Willard G. Plentl to November, 11 April 1967.

7 Letter, November to William F. McKee, 12 April 1967; and letter, Johnston to November, 14 April 1967.

8 Arven H. Saunders to November, 24 April 1967.

9 Memorandum, Casey to Frank Taylor, "Proposal for the Display of NASM Study Collection," 24 September 1969.

10 Letter, T. Murray Toomey to Frederick C. Durant III, 6 November 1969.

11 Letter, David T. Walker to Members, Dulles International Development Study Commission, 20 April 1971, with enclosure, "Minutes, Dulles International Airport Development Commission, Dulles International Airport, Virginia, April 8, 1971."

12 Letter, Michael Collins to November, 8 March 1974.

13 Memorandum, Donald S. Lopez to Collins, "Near and Long Term Plans for Storage," 9 November 1977.

14 NASM staff paper, "Why We Need an Airfield Wing," circa 1983; the six airfields surveyed were Washington National, Andrews Air Force Base, Baltimore-Washington International, Glenn L. Martin, Hagerstown Fairchild, and Dulles International. In 1981, the Museum also examined Beltsville Airport on the grounds of the National Agricultural Research Center in Maryland but found the facility in the process of being demolished. In 1983, Berkeley County officials offered the Eastern West Virginia Regional Airport as a site worth considering. In 1985, the National Park Service asked the Smithsonian to also consider Floyd Bennett Field in New York, a site that was also rejected based on the size of the existing hangars and the distance from Washington, D.C.

15 Memorandum, Marc Mayer to Rita Jordan, "Proposed Dulles Facility Justification," 7 July 1983.

Chapter 2

1 Douglas Wonderlic, "Feasibility Study for National Air and Space Museum Wing at Dulles International Airport (NASM-Dulles Feasibility Study)", 3 November 1983, rev. 15 May 1984.

2 Washington Dulles Airport, "Final Technical Report, Master Plan Update, Washington Dulles Airport," September 1985, 132–133; memo, Paul A. Hanle to Donald S. Lopez, "List for Dulles Facility," 13 September 1983; and "National Air and Space Museum Development Concept for Storage and Exhibit Facility at Dulles International Airport," circa September 1983.

3 In February 1984, Senators Goldwater, Garn, and Sasser submitted authorization legislation S.-2272, and Representative Mineta and others submitted H.R.-4714, neither of which passed. In June 1985, Senators Goldwater, Garn, Glenn, Trible, and Warner submitted S.-1311, and in September 1985 Representatives Mineta, Boland, Conte, Wolf, Parris, and Fuqua introduced H.R.-3403, neither of which passed.

4 Dewberry and Davis, "Concept Study, National Air and Space Museum Dulles Wing/Phase 1," September 1985; and Leo J. Schefer and Thomas G. Morr, "Initial Phase Funding Proposal," 15 October 1985. The Council valued the contributed study at $400,000.

5 Of the National Air and Space Museum (NASM) team, Don Lopez, Al Bachmeier, and Lin Ezell would still be on staff and actively working on the project when the Steven F. Udvar-Hazy Center opened in 2003.

6 Dewberry and Davis, "Concept Study, National Air and Space Museum Dulles Wing/Phase 1," September 1985, 10–12.

7 Dewberry and Davis, "Concept Study, National Air and Space Museum Dulles Wing/Phase 1," September 1985, 50–54, 59; and Air and Space Heritage Council, Inc., "National Air and Space Museum Dulles Wing, Volunteered Conceptual Phase: July 1, 1985–July 1, 1986," circa July 1986.

8 NASM, "The Dulles Wing of NASM," February 1986; and NASM, "The Dulles Wing of NASM," September 1987. In 1986, developer Bahman Batmanghelidj proposed that a space exposition complex be built near Dulles, which would include the NASM facility.

9 Letter, Phillip K. Reiss to Marilyn Jordan Taylor, "Planning for the National Air and Space Museum Extension," 29 April 1988; and letter, Schefer to Martin O. Harwit, 19 January 1988. The cost of the Skidmore, Owings & Merrill study was $90,844.

10 Steven Soter, "NASM Extension Concepts," 20 July 1988.

11 Skidmore, Owings & Merrill (SOM), "Presentation to the Adams Committee," 10 August 1988; SOM, "Planning for the National Air and Space Museum Extension," September 1988. The Garber staff contracted with senior museum professional David Scott to prepare a series of reports that better documented and quantified the conditions at Garber and requirements for the collections at Dulles in 1988–89.

12 Memo, Ross Simons to Wonderlic, "Draft Report for NASM Extension," 12 August 1988; Nancy D. Suttenfield to Phillip K. Reiss, "Draft Planning Study for the NASM Extension," 12 August 1988; and memo, Margaret Gaynor to Robert Mc. Adams, "NASM/SOM Study," 19 August 1988.

13 Memo, Adams to NASM Extension Working Group, "8/23/88 Meeting with Skidmore, Owings, Merrill," 23 August 1988.

14 Also in 1988–89, in addition to the Baltimore airport site, the Museum was asked to consider sites in Prince George's County, Md., and one senior NASM staff member reconsidered the idea of locating the complex in Anacostia, near Washington, using barges to relocate aircraft to a waterfront site. San Antonio, Tex., and St. Petersburg-Clearwater, Fla., offered sites in 1990. Moffett Naval Station, Calif., weighed in in 1991. There were numerous offers in 1992: the Baltimore Development Corporation suggested the city's inner harbor area; supporters of Marine Corps Air Station, Tustin, Calif., wrote offering facilities; Pittsburgh made a pitch; as did Houston; from Florida, the Piper Aircraft Facility was suggested; Carswell Air Force Base was offered from Texas.

15 Hellmuth, Obata + Kassabaum (HOK), "The National Air and Space Museum Extension: Site Evaluation, Planning and Phasing," 15 December 1989. $350,000 had been earmarked for site evaluation and master planning by Congress.

16 News release, Smithsonian Institution (SI), "Site for National Air and Space Museum Extension Announced," 29 January 1990.

17 Harwit, "Assumptions on the Extension," 19 October 1990.

18 Wendy Stephens, "Planning for the Proposed Extension," 23 April 1992, in response to formal questions from Congressional committee staff. See also note 14 above.

19 News release, SI, "Background Fact Sheet, Extension of the National Air and Space Museum," March 1993; and news release, SI, "President Clinton Signs Legislation to Establish National Air and Space Museum Extension," 3 August 1993.

20 Memo, A. Bradley Mims to Gwen Crider, "Description of the NASM Extension," 1 September 1993.

21 HOK, "The National Air and Space Museum Extension Master Plan Space Requirement Program," October 1993 and updated in October 1996.

22 HOK, "The National Air and Space Museum Extension Master Plan Report on Building Criteria/Cost Parameters," 31 January 1995.

23 Dames & Moore, "Final Assessment for Proposed National Air and Space Museum Dulles Center, Washington Dulles International Airport, Fairfax County, Virginia," 24 February 1998.

24 Harrison Price Company, "Revised Final Report, Attendance Planning Update for the NASM Extension, Dulles International Airport," September 1996.

25 HOK, "NASM Extension Master Plan Phase, Concept Design, Draft Final Report," 16 May 1996.

26 Statement, J. William Gadsby, "Testimony before the Subcommittee on Government Management, Information, and Technology, Committee on Government Reform and Oversight, and the Committee on House Oversight, House of Representatives, Smithsonian Institution, Care of National Air and Space Museum Aircraft," 25 September 1996.

27 Contractually, HOK's work officially transitioned from planning to design with the execution of an option to amend HOK's contract in October 1996. HOK assisted the Smithsonian with securing two external approvals during the late 1990s, as part of their contract work. The Commission of Fine Arts, chaired by J. Carter Brown, endorsed the design in early 1998. The National Capital Planning Commission approved it during the spring of 1998.

Chapter 3

1 Hellmuth, Obata + Kassabaum (HOK), "The National Air and Space Museum Extension Master Plan, Risk Assessment Report," 10 October 1995.

2 Dames & Moore, "1995/1996 Wetland Delineation of Smithsonian-National Air and Space Museum Extension Site, Dulles Aiport, Fairfax County, Virginia," 10 June 1996.

3 HOK, "Environmental Assessment for Proposed National Air and Space Museum Dulles Center, Washington Dulles International Airport, Fairfax County, Virginia," 10 March 1997, 5-2 to 5-7.

4 "Memorandum of Understanding," signed by Smithsonian Institution Secretary I. Michael Heyman and Virginia Governor George Allen, 22 April 1996. This document is a follow-up to Governor Gerald L. Baliles' letter of intent to Secretary Robert Mc. Adams, 15 December 1989. The formal MOU provided financial information and budget targets for the assistance package.

5 Press release, National Air and Space Museum, "National Air and Space Museum Receives $60 million Pledge for its Dulles Center," 7 October 1999.

6 This chapter was based primarily on a series of reports usually produced monthly by the Project Management Division of the Office of Physical Plant. The first such report was titled "National Air and Space Museum Dulles Center Monthly Report," December 1996/January 1997. With a catch-up report covering the period February–July 2000, the title changed to reflect the new name of the project: "National Air and Space Museum Steven F. Udvar-Hazy Center Project Management Report." These documents reviewed schedule, budget, critical path items, design progress and problems, and external issues.

Chapter 4

Primary references for this chapter are monthly progress reports produced by the Office of Physical Plant, which became the Office of Facilities Engineering and Operations, and the author's recollections of the period.

1 Smithsonian Institution (SI), Office of Contracting (OCon), "Steven F. Udvar-Hazy Center Dulles NASM Bidders List 5/00, Solicitation/RFP Number T0036SOL0021," rev. 12 June 2000.

2 Memo, OCon to Prospective Offeror, "Request for Proposal No. T0036SOL0021—Construction of the National Air and Space Museum, Steven F. Udvar-Hazy Center," 10 May 2000, with the RFP, dated 10 May 2000, attached.

3 Memos, Melinda Humphry Becker to Lin Ezell, "Addendum to the Contract for Construction," 22 May 2000 and 9 June 2000.

4 Memo, OCon to Prospective Offeror, "Request for Proposal," 10 May 2000, with RFP, p. 6. The technical team members were Derek Ross, chair (non-voting), Sheryl Kolasinski, Melinda Humphry Becker, George Golden, Vince Cogliano, and Lin Ezell. They were assisted by Walter Urbanek of HOK, Paul Dickens of Parsons Brinckerhoff, and Al Bachmeier and William "Jake" Jacobs of NASM.

5 E-mail, Ezell to Jack Dailey, "Phasing Construction," 30 October 2000; and memo, Lloyd McGill to Paulette Pressley, "Items for Discussion with Contractors," 16 November 2000.

6 Memo, Sheila Burke to Members of the Executive Committee, SI Board of Regents, "Update on the Steven F. Udvar-Hazy Center Project," 23 March 2001; memo, Jim Hobbins to Sudeep Anand, "Regents' Executive Committee Approval of Udvar-Hazy Construction," 28 March 2001; and SI contract T0136CC10276, 29 March 2001.

7 Hensel Phelps Construction Co., "Employee Safety and Health Handbook," August 2001, inside cover.

Index

Notes
1. Illustrations are indicated by *italic* page numbers. There may also be textual references on these pages.
2. Source notes are *not* included in this index.